JOAN K. McMICHAEL M.B., Ch.B.

HANDICAP

A Study of
Physically Handicapped Children
and their Families

University of Pittsburgh Press

FIRST PUBLISHED IN GREAT BRITAIN 1971 BY
STAPLES PRESS LTD
COPYRIGHT © JOAN K. MCMICHAEL 1971
ALL RIGHTS RESERVED
LIBRARY OF CONGRESS CATALOG CARD NUMBER 77-189858
ISBN 0-8229-1106-X

PRINTED IN GREAT BRITAIN BY
FLETCHER AND SON LTD, NORWICH

To the Courage of
Handicapped Children

JACK TIZARD

Professor of Child Development in the University of London

IN THIS short monograph Dr McMichael reports the findings of a study dealing with the personal and social circumstances of fifty severely handicapped children, all of whom were pupils in a special primary school for the physically handicapped. She was well equipped to undertake her investigation in that she was the school doctor at the particular school in which the inquiry was carried out, and so was well known to the children, the teachers and to many of the parents. Dr McMichael gives a vivid picture of the difficulties and problems faced by children with severe physical handicaps, and of the courage which many of them showed in meeting these. The problems of parents were no less daunting, and for many families little was being done—though there was often much that could have in fact been done—to help them. It was clear that many parents would have welcomed help long before the children even started school.

I see the chief value of Dr McMichael's survey in the description she gives of the lives of a particular group of handicapped children and their families. Teachers, caseworkers and doctors who are concerned with the handicapped can read her account with profit, for it will make them better informed about, and more sensitive to, the needs of the children, and the families whom they serve.

Because it is concerned with a single institution and with a small and possibly unrepresentative group of handicapped children, a study such as this offers possibilities to the investigator which are different from, but which for some purposes may be more valuable than, those offered by national or large-scale surveys. There is an intimacy about case studies which is invariably lacking in studies of larger samples. The information obtained—in this instance by a sympathetic and well-informed doctor who is known to, and trusted by, the people she is writing about—is likely to be more detailed than is that secured in larger inquiries, which usually have as a primary purpose the establishment of normative data

7

relating to the prevalence of handicaps. It is true that in case studies there are inherent difficulties in securing representative data, but biases are not necessarily eliminated by being magnified a thousand-fold; and to the handicapped child and his family, suffering is neither more nor less real whether it occurs in other families or not. For a case study such as this therefore, a 'control' group would serve little purpose; and even to know the comparative frequency of various problems is perhaps of less importance than is the knowledge that for the families studied medical, educational, social and material problems occur in all their complexity in a high proportion of cases. Moreover, these problems are by no means confined to physically handicapped children and their families. One of the striking findings that has emerged from investigations made of children with other types of handicap—mental subnormality, psychiatric disorder, epilepsy, severe educational backwardness, for example, no less than physical handicap—is the similarity between the difficulties they and their families experience.

Dr McMichael confesses that there were occasions when she found it difficult to assess the validity of some of the information she collected. Of course she has found, as others have, that perceived facts don't always agree. Parents may perceive a child's problem differently from teachers, and a doctor or caseworker may disagree with both parents and teachers and with each other. So a study such as this bristles with methodological problems which students will find it profitable to discuss. None the less the main conclusions emerge clearly.

It would be valuable to know how these children have progressed during the years that have elapsed since this study was carried out. I hope Dr McMichael will have the time and the occasion to carry out a follow-up study which would add another dimension to her work.

AUTHOR'S ACKNOWLEDGEMENTS

THIS BOOK is based on a survey of the problems of fifty handicapped children and their families. The children attended a small London County Council (now Inner London Education Authority) primary day school for physically handicapped children, and the LCC gave me permission, as the school doctor, to undertake the study. The Council also accorded me one half-day per week over a period of eighteen months (1960 and 1961) for the interview schedules on which the survey is based. The interviews were conducted with one or both parents or guardians, in their own homes.

It is with pleasure that I acknowledge my gratitude to the late Dr J. A. Scott, Medical Officer of Health for London, for the facilities to carry out the survey, and to the Principal School Medical Officer, Dr Denis Pirrie, and the Chief Statistician of the Public Health Statistical Section, Mr Shaddick, for their assistance and advice.

I am especially grateful to Professor Jack Tizard, of the Social Psychiatry Research Unit of the Medical Research Council, for his help and guidance in the initial planning of the survey and in the designing of the standard interview schedule; for allowing me to use the teachers' questionnaire constructed for the National Survey of the Health and Development of Children (May 1959); and for his counsel at every stage of the work.

I am also happy to express my gratitude to Dr I. B. Pless, Assistant Professor of Pediatrics, University of Rochester School of Medicine and Dentistry, New York, who so generously gave his time and energy to a comprehensive revision of the final draft of the book, and from whom I have received invaluable advice and encouragement.

My thanks are due also to the headmistress and staff of the school for their cooperation in completing the teachers' questionnaire for each child, and to my colleague, Dr Faith Spicer, for her contribution in completing five interview schedules for independent assessment.

In quoting individual cases to illustrate general problems, I have altered names and some of the external circumstances, in order to disguise the identity of the children and their parents. If by any chance a

Author's Acknowledgements

mother should read the book and recognize herself, I offer her my apologies, and ask her to understand that what she has told me has been invaluable for medical research and will help other parents who are faced with similar problems.

Among the many other people who have assisted me in this investigation I would mention in particular the school sister, the parents, without whose cooperation the survey would have been impossible, and the members of my family, who patiently bore with my preoccupation and gave me encouragement and practical suggestions throughout the course of the work.

J.K.MCM.

CONTENTS

Contents

HANDICAP

CHAPTER I

The Scope of the Survey

'To possess a handicap is to be different from the majority. There is a deep need in human beings to be one with and of the community, and anything which prevents one from doing the things which others do tends to isolate one . . . it affects their relationships with other people . . . it affects other people's relationships with them.'

JOHN D. KERSHAW, *Handicapped Children*

BACKGROUND TO THE STUDY

ANYONE who has worked with handicapped children will immediately recognize and understand the truth of these words, and echo them from his own experiences. The complexity of the interacting problems is now becoming more generally appreciated. We are beginning to realize that *a physical handicap, of itself, constitutes an emotional hazard and sooner or later will become an emotional challenge both for the child and his family.* The handicap will involve the family from time to time in crises which they can either surmount, thus strengthening their own personalities and relationships, or evade, so weakening and distorting them. These crises and the problems that give·rise to them continue throughout the infancy and school life of the handicapped child, and so long as the handicap exists.

When I was appointed the school medical officer for a small primary day school for physically handicapped children, I was soon made aware that the children and their families had many pressing needs in addition to those of medical supervision. As a result of constant discussions with parents, teachers, caseworkers, physiotherapists and others, I began to try to see each child as an individual, with his own particular set of problems, and not merely as 'a case of paralysis following poliomyelitis', or whatever the diagnosis might be.

From the teachers I learned about the children's special educational difficulties, attributable to the loss of school time and continuity as a result of illness, admissions to hospital and other kinds of treatment, and to the effects of these experiences on their ability to concentrate. They also explained the learning difficulties that derived from the loss or impairment of educational skills, such as speech, hearing or muscular coordination. We discussed the children's emotional difficulties, the strains and anxieties arising from their efforts to adjust themselves to their handicaps, and the way in which all this affected their ability to learn.

From the trained social workers I began to understand some of the problems of the families: the reaction of the parents when they were first told of their child's handicap; their feelings of anxiety and guilt about the cause of the handicap; their fears about future pregnancies; the attitude of other members of the family who might find it difficult to accept the extra time and attention given to the handicapped child; and the many limitations and sacrifices imposed by the handicap on each of them.

The following example will illustrate some of these points. Brian was a Rhesus-negative baby transfused at birth. When he was three days old his father was told he might be mentally defective, blind or deaf, or all three. The infant showed little response and had very little muscular control. He was difficult to feed and although the mother attended a welfare clinic regularly, her son was believed to be grossly defective until he was a year old, when he was referred to a children's hospital. He was diagnosed as a severe cerebral palsy (spastic) and referred to another hospital specializing in this condition.

The parents were again told that the child was completely mentally defective and no treatment was advised. Nevertheless they continued to attend the first hospital for physiotherapy and although muscular coordination was slow to develop, there was steady progress. The child was later found to be highly intelligent, although deaf and suffering from a severe speech defect in addition to his spastic paralysis.

In spite of their overwhelming anxieties and disappointments, and their regrets at the loss of the vital first twelve months of training in infancy, his sensible and devoted parents succeeded in helping Brian to accept his handicap and to remain a happy and courageous child. Although still unable to walk unaided, he is now winning obstacle races on his tricycle at a deaf unit in a residential school for spastic children.

I had frequent discussions about how and when parents should first be told that their child was handicapped; how they could be supported and helped to accept the handicap, and to make the necessary adjustments, both in the early critical days and weeks, when they first have to face relatives and friends with a baby who 'has something wrong with him', and later through the inevitable crises associated with the handicap.

School naturally presents a handicapped child and his parents with a new set of problems. For some parents the initial difficulty may lie in coming to terms with the fact that their child may have to go to a school for handicapped children. Not only must they now accept official recognition that their child is handicapped and not like other children, but they will have to accept the fact that he will be mixing with other children who may be more severely handicapped and more obviously 'not normal'. One mother, whose child suffered from severe haemophilia and therefore looked quite normal, was never really able to accept her son's 'being with other children who are afflicted'. There is a natural fear of the effect on a child of being with other children who are more severely handicapped than he is himself; in fact, the child usually tends to accept the situation much more easily than his parents and will quite often 'adopt' a friend with a greater disability and enjoy helping and looking after him.

At school the need for teamwork and coordination in the care of a handicapped child soon becomes obvious because of the large number of agencies involved: the hospital authorities, the visiting consultants, the child's own doctor, the social welfare agencies, the school authorities and, most important of all, the parents.

The parents are, and must always be, the single most important factor in the care of a handicapped child. They must take full responsibility for supervising him and carrying out his treatment, day in and day out, year in and year out. If they are unable or unwilling to cooperate, the best treatment can be made ineffective: appliances may be lost or broken; a partially paralysed limb may remain unused for long hours and during whole weekends or holidays; faulty postures or movements may remain uncorrected; crutches may be used to swing on instead of for learning to walk properly. Worst of all, a child may be discouraged from making the efforts necessary to help his recovery or to bring about the best possible adjustment to his handicap. So much depends on the attitude of the parents that it is essential to secure their understanding and cooperation at every stage. This may be difficult or impossible to achieve in a busy outpatient clinic with constantly changing personnel.

This survey was undertaken in the first place as an attempt to see the handicapped child in the round, observing him from many different aspects and taking account of the various kinds of problems that can affect him and his family. Such an approach raises, inevitably, the question of coordination. Who should be responsible for the overall supervision and care of the child? Should it be the family doctor? What part does he play in the treatment and supervision of the handicapped child? How successful are any attempts to achieve teamwork in the interests of the child? What is, or should be, the role of the school doctor? In short, is there some lack of coordination? Where are the gaps and how can they be filled?

Furthermore, is there any continuity in the support of the handicapped child and his family from the first agonizing days when the handicap is recognized, whether it be congenital or acquired, through the periods of the parents' adjustment and the child's adjustment when he is older; and through the recurring crises of hospitalization and adaptation to the limitations imposed by the handicap at home and school, and for the future? Is there anyone who can give this continuity of support? Can the family doctor give the necessary time? Or the Health visitor, who is in contact with the handicapped baby and his mother when they come out of hospital, but who will lose touch with them when the child goes to school? Should there be a special agency, with caseworkers trained in the problems of handicapped children and their families? There are voluntary agencies such as the Invalid Children's Aid Association. Do they fulfil this role? How far are they available and how widely are they used?

AIMS AND METHODS

With these questions in mind I consulted Professor Jack Tizard of the Social Psychiatry Research Unit of the Medical Research Council, who was at the time completing a survey of the problems of the mentally handicapped and their families (Tizard and Grad, 1961). With his help and cooperation I was able to work out a standard interview schedule of 156 questions based on the one he had used but adapted to the special problems of physically handicapped children. This survey questionnaire (Appendix I) was designed primarily to provide information on aspects of medical supervision and on the psychological, social and educational problems associated with the physical handicap.

To provide an independent assessment of at least some of the children's problems, I secured Professor Tizard's agreement to my use of the teachers' questionnaire that had been prepared for the National Survey of the Health and Development of Children (May 1959) (Appendix II).

These two questionnaires, completed independently by the school doctor and the class teacher for each of the fifty children, provided the main source of material for the survey. Additional material was obtained from the medical records and from the reports of the caseworkers from the Invalid Children's Aid Association, members of the School Care Committee. Furthermore, the routine medical work in school included discussions from time to time, in which those concerned with the children's health and progress took part, i.e. visiting consultants, teachers, the school sister, physiotherapists, caseworkers, members of the child guidance units where appropriate and, of course, the parents.

The object of the survey was to build up a comprehensive picture of the problems of the child and his family in relation to his handicap.

A preliminary study of three handicapped children and their families was made by me in 1959 to check and adapt the interview schedule. The amended schedule was then discussed and agreed with the statistical section of the London County Council, whose help was enlisted for the analysis of the results.

The survey was originally planned to cover the fifty-nine children who were on the school roll in June 1960 and, in addition, two of the three children in the preliminary study, who had left the school in the intervening period. Five of these children were, however, transferred to residential schools or schools in other areas during the survey, and were replaced by five new admissions. The children were taken in order of convenience (school-leavers first), with the intention of interviewing all sixty-one; arrangements for the interviews were made with parents either when they attended a routine medical examination, or by letter.

Fifty schedules were completed by me between July 1960 and July 1961 from interviews with one or both parents or guardians in the child's home and supplemented from the medical records. The survey was actually terminated when fifty of the sixty-one cases had been interviewed, for reasons of time and convenience of analysis.

In five cases, interviews using the survey questionnaire were repeated independently by a second school medical officer, Dr Faith Spicer. She had no previous knowledge of the children concerned, or of their parents, and saw them without reference to the medical records. In spite of the obvious difficulties inherent in two such different approaches, the answers to over 75 per cent of the questions showed agreement. The disagreements, apart from a few minor differences in the interpretation of 'not applicable' and 'don't know', appeared due to the mothers' different responses to someone they knew well and to a complete stranger. The differences were most marked where the mothers were suffering the deepest emotional distress, as in the case of one mother whose child had an inoperable brain tumour. This mother admitted her anxiety and depression to the school doctor, but denied them to the unknown doctor, to whom she expressed unlimited confidence based on her religious beliefs. Moreover, previous experience had shown her to be subject to considerable swings of mood between hope and despair.

During this same period the class teachers completed the teachers' questionnaire for forty-eight of the fifty children, and these were approved by the headmistress. One of the remaining cases, who had been in the preliminary study, had left and the class teacher felt that she did not remember him sufficiently clearly; the other child had been too short a time in the class for the teacher to form an opinion before he left unexpectedly.

The answers relating to school absenteeism were subsequently checked with the school register and the time spent by the children in speech, occupational therapy and physiotherapy was also confirmed from school records. It soon became clear that mothers were quite unable to remember the exact number and dates of hospital admissions and discharges, especially where these were numerous. In the case of some children, those with haemophilia for instance, who had been admitted to hospital twenty to thirty times and more, and often to several different hospitals, the records of hospital admissions were incomplete. Admissions and discharges for all the children were therefore checked where possible with the records officers of all the hospitals concerned.

During the course of the investigation, it became apparent that the indications of failure to make a satisfactory adjustment, on the part of some of the children and their parents, needed further study. The rate of referral for child guidance was high (24 per cent compared with 8 per cent in the three pilot schemes in ordinary schools referred to in the report of the Underwood Committee to the Ministry of Education in 1955), and the number of parents, both mothers and fathers, under treatment for anxiety states was striking.

Since similar signs were present in varying degrees among many other children and parents who were receiving no specific treatment, it became necessary to devise some method of assessing the severity of the emotional strains and the degree of failure to adjust. With Professor Tizard's help, I therefore designed some scoring standards to measure these emotional strains in the children and their parents. Those for the children were based on responses to both the survey and the teachers' questionnaires, selected according to the groups of symptoms and headings given in the Under-wood Report. Those for the parents were based largely on answers selected from the survey questionnaire, but included four responses from the teachers' questionnaire as possible indications of parental attitudes.

The whole of this material, including the scoring standards, was then submitted to the statistical section of the London County Council for analysis.

A full report on the survey was submitted to the Medical Officer of Health for London in 1962. The various recommendations made are currently under consideration. The present volume offers the substance of this report to a wider public.

CHAPTER 2

The School Setting

ORGANIZATION AND FACILITIES

THE SCHOOL in which the survey took place is a small primary day school for physically handicapped boys and girls in the London area. It is one of the oldest of eleven such schools in London, and has been adapted to meet the special needs of physically handicapped children from both the medical and the educational points of view.

The newer schools for physically handicapped children have been specially built for the purpose to the latest designs and in beautiful surroundings. Their modern equipment may include a heated swimming-pool on the premises which can be used by the children all the year round.

Our school, however, is small and rather out of date. It is housed on the ground floor of a typical four-storey London school built in 1870. It is in a street of rather respectable small houses, next to a poorer and more overcrowded area which contains a large coal storage dump. The other three floors of the school are used by an ordinary primary day school for the children of the neighbourhood. These children have separate entrances and playgrounds, and usually mix with the handicapped children only when they invite them to a school concert or garden party.

Although the building is old and was never designed for its present purpose, the school, like its more modern counterparts, aims to provide the conditions which will enable each physically handicapped child to develop to his or her full capacity. The atmosphere is purposeful and happy, and the children, for the most part, appear to enjoy their school life in spite of their disabilities and difficulties.

Special buses, with attendants, bring the children to school each day, collecting them from a wide catchment area covering four London boroughs. The staff includes a full-time nursing Sister who supervises the children's health and gives any treatment needed. A team of four physiotherapists from a local children's hospital comes four times a week to carry out the physiotherapy required, by agreement with the hospitals concerned, and a speech therapist twice a week for the children with speech defects. The children are thus able to get the treatment needed while in school, instead of losing school time travelling to and from hospital.

The classes are small and each child receives a good deal of attention. On the other hand, the wide range of age and ability in a single class, and the time lost by each child for hospital attendance, illness or treatment, must make it difficult to plan a syllabus. For this reason, even smaller classes or, best of all, some opportunity for individual teaching would be welcomed by the staff.

Children come to school at five years old, or sometimes earlier by special arrangement. The infant class here has overflowed into a 'temporary' pavilion-like classroom in the playground, rather conveniently located next door to Sister in the medical room, where the children go of their own accord if they feel unwell, or for extra rest. The infants' pavilion looks out on to the playground, which includes a big lawn and garden where the children can play in the summer.

There are three other classrooms and a hall. The hall is used, among other things, for physical education, which these children enjoy even more than normal children. To their endless delight some Essex equipment has been provided quite recently. This consists of climbing ribs, bars and frames, which they can help to set up quickly. Exercises on these are enjoyed, within each one's limited capacity, by many of the most handicapped children. Many of the older children also go swimming each week at the local baths—a Mecca to which every seven-year-old aspires. To do P.E. and to go swimming like children in ordinary schools boosts morale—in spite of the difficulties of getting dressed and undressed, and the assistance needed in the water.

The school has a dining-room (a converted classroom) where the Sister and the school attendants are ready to help those children who have difficulties in feeding themselves. In the large kitchen, cook takes a personal interest in the children's needs and sends in minute portions for those who have to be tempted to eat. There is also a large suitably equipped room for physiotherapy and various staff rooms.

The whole school is on one floor, with a ramp leading down to the infants' pavilion and the medical room. The children on crutches or in chairs can manage to get about without much difficulty and there are always volunteers to wheel the chairborne.

Handicap

There are usually between fifty and sixty children on the school roll. Some who have mild or temporary handicaps, such as fractures, stay only a term or two whilst on crutches—the aim is to get them back to ordinary school as soon as possible. Most of the children admitted at five years stay until eleven and go on to a secondary day school for the physically handicapped.

EDUCATIONAL TRANSFERS DURING THE STUDY PERIOD

Table I shows the number of children transferred during the course of the survey to other types of school or tuition.

TABLE I

Educational transfers during the study period

Type of transfer	No. of children
To secondary school for the physically handicapped	7
To ordinary school	6
To boarding school for the physically handicapped	3
To home tuition	1
To day open-air school	1

Four of the six children who returned to ordinary schools were mild cases of poliomyelitis involving one leg. The fifth child, with a tuberculous spine, made a complete recovery. The sixth child was interesting from another point of view. At four months he was considered to have a ventricular septal defect and in due course came to the physically handicapped school. He was referred for further assessment at seven years and, following cardiac catheterization, the diagnosis was revised and the murmur was considered innocent. The child returned to ordinary school, where he was able to work off the surplus energy previously an embarrassment to all concerned.

Three children were transferred to boarding schools for the physically handicapped for different reasons. Vernon's mother had to move back to Wales, because of domestic and housing difficulties in London. Since

24

there was no day school for physically handicapped children locally and physiotherapy was difficult to arrange, Vernon, who was a mild ataxic paraplegia, was admitted to a boarding school. Brian was a child with athetoid paraplegia and a severe hearing loss; he was offered a place in the new deaf unit of a residential school for spastics. The third child, Hubert, was transferred to a residential school to relieve the strain on his widowed mother, suffering from severe depression and anxiety, and to enable her to attend regularly for psychiatric treatment. The regular regime and peaceful atmosphere of the country boarding school also benefited the child, who was suffering from Fallot's tetralogy, with symptoms of heart failure and cretinism.

George, the child who received home tuition, had severe haemophilia. He developed poliomyelitis at two and a half, and one leg was completely paralysed. His case highlights the difficulties facing families who move to new housing estates outside the London area. There was no day school for physically handicapped children on the estate to which the family moved and the parents refused to consider a boarding school. The only available alternative was home tuition four times a week for one hour. Other serious problems that arose in this family with four haemophilic boys are discussed in detail in Chapter 5.

Quintin, the boy transferred to a day open-air school, was a withdrawn, depressed child with severe haemophilia. His mother, who experienced great difficulty in adjusting to his handicap, was quite unable to tolerate the presence of other 'afflicted' children in the handicapped school and finally, after pressing for home tuition, agreed to accept the day open-air school, at least temporarily, until he was 'able to look after himself'.

THE ROLE OF THE SCHOOL DOCTOR AND THE SCHOOL TEAM

The role of the school doctor is to supervise the health, welfare and treatment of each child. This involves a concern for the *whole* child—the physical and educational aspects, as well as 'the intellectual, emotional and social aspects' referred to by Apley and MacKeith (1962). The school doctor must also act as a liaison between all the different agencies that are involved in the care of the child to ensure the necessary teamwork in the approach to his problems.

On the *medical* side, the most consistently available member of the team is the school Sister, who works full time in the school and therefore knows each child intimately and can give continuous supervision. It is to the school Sister that parents write when they are anxious about some aspect of the child's health or treatment, and letters and messages go back and forth through bus attendants or by telephone.

Every child is under the care of a hospital consultant and, in addition, children with cardiac or orthopaedic conditions are visited once a term by the Council's consultants.

A speech therapist attends the school to help the numerous children whose handicaps include a speech defect. It is evident that regular individual contact with a sympathetic adult in the course of such treatment has a therapeutic value in itself and encourages the child to use the powers of communication he is being trained to develop. The visiting team of physiotherapists, already mentioned, and an occupational therapist complete the medical facilities provided.

The teaching staff, the headmistress and the class teachers are constantly concerned with the health as well as the educational progress of the children, since the two are so closely interdependent in a school for physically handicapped children. Their day-to-day observation of the children and their understanding of each child's special difficulties in coping with a particular handicap in the class situation can be invaluable to the doctor. They also help to assess a child's progress and the effects of the various components of his treatment—always providing there are adequate opportunities for the exchange of information between teaching and medical personnel.

The recent appointment to the school of an educational psychologist was a welcome addition to the team. Her routine assessments of the children, together with specialist advice on particular problems, proved a great help in relation to both learning difficulties and behaviour problems. Unfortunately, her rather infrequent visits did not coincide with the one morning every two or three weeks on which school medical examinations were held, and it was not easy for the doctor and the educational psychologist—each with a full, or overfull timetable—to make time and opportunity for an exchange of views and experiences. If meetings have to be arranged out of school hours, without the relevant case records at hand, it is unlikely that the best use can be made of the complementary approaches.

The school situation often appears to have a therapeutic value of its own, and there tends to be something rather special about the atmosphere of a small school for physically handicapped children. This may be partly because the classes are small, and there is time and opportunity to know every child and his individual problems. It may arise also, in part, because most adults have deep feelings of sympathy for children whose handicaps deprive them of so many of the normal joys of childhood. But there is no doubt that it is largely due to the reactions of the children themselves to their school.

Nowadays, most normal five-year-olds tend to regard school as a joyous adventure. For handicapped children, even if they are nervous on arrival, school may open a new world. Many of them may have felt isolated at home—unable to play in the street or to join in ordinary children's games. It is difficult for them to make friends with children who can do so much more and who naturally want to be more active. Thus, in ordinary life the handicapped child must often feel the odd man out or, worse still, an oddity. Many of the mothers spoke of their constantly recurring pain and anger when people turned to stare at their handicapped child and made audible comments or gave loud explanations to their inquiring offspring.

Here in school, perhaps for the first time in their lives (excluding periods in hospital where the atmosphere is out of the ordinary anyway), the handicapped children are the 'normal' ones. Everyone has a handicap, and it is taken for granted. No one pays particular attention to it (unless help is needed) and nothing is looked on as out of the ordinary.

A severe congenital heart lesion, Case 12, illustrates some of the points made. Bertie was a boy of eight and a half, an only child, and grossly overweight. His parents were so disturbed and anxious that they were quite unable to talk about him and his difficulties to each other except in the presence of a third person, the doctor or the caseworker. Before Bertie came to the school for physically handicapped children he had attended, at the parents' urgent insistence, an ordinary infants' school, although he had to be taken there in a push-chair. It was only when he moved up to the junior school and finally became quite unable to cope with the stairs that they reluctantly agreed to his going to a day school for the physically handicapped.

His mother found it hard, at first, to accept the other handicapped and crippled children and asked him if he did not miss his friends at the other school. His shattering reply was: 'I didn't have any friends there—I couldn't run fast enough.' He did not find it easy to settle, however, and matters became much worse when the cardiologist told the parents that Bertie was unlikely to survive adolescence. His father's not unnatural reaction was: 'Why should I force him to go to school then? There's no point in it.' By the time that his mother, with the help of the caseworker, had persuaded the father to agree to the boy's coming to school again, Bertie was thoroughly miserable and uncooperative. The teacher's rather terse comment was: 'He wants more than his share of attention and consideration.'

The large-sized chip on Bertie's shoulder caused him—and the teaching staff—considerable difficulties for some time, but at the end of two or three terms he began to get his own problems into perspective. His physical condition improved—helped by strict dieting and loss of weight —and the tensions at home were, at least to some extent, relieved by the weekly visits of the caseworker. At last the longed-for day arrived when he was allowed to go swimming with the school. When finally he was made school captain, he not only shouldered his responsibilities with great determination but lost a good deal of the preoccupation with his own difficulties that had obviously made his life such a burden when he first arrived.

One other typical scene springs to mind: a sunny dinner hour in the playground; two close friends, severe spastics, neither able to stand or speak clearly, sit, each on a mat wielding a cricket bat with a willing circle of children bowling and fielding for them; all deeply absorbed in their own version of a Test Match.

LINKS WITH THE FAMILY AND HOME-VISITING

In considering the health and welfare of any child at school the doctor must know the basic facts about the child's background. Every child is the product of his heredity and environment and the key to an understanding of his individual problems lies in knowing something of his home and family relationships. If such knowledge is important for the psychosomatic approach to the child in an ordinary school, it is absolutely essential in respect of the child at a school for the physically handicapped.

As the school medical service is at present organized, and in order to avoid any overlap or complications with the family doctor service, the school doctor must normally rely for his information on the reports of various agencies visiting the home. These will consist in the first place of the written reports of Health Visitors, covering the first five years of the child's life. The new abbreviated record forms, however, leave little space for any but the most brief and formal of comments.

Current reports on home conditions of children in London schools are given by members of the voluntary School Care Committee Organization who attend the school medical examinations. The individual attending, however, may or may not be the one who has visited the home. The value of the reports naturally varies with the training and skill of those who make them, and according to whether they are given first hand or compiled from notes made by another social worker.

In any ordinary school these arrangements may give rise to difficulties. In a school for handicapped children, where the problems and emotional complications are so much greater, they often prove inadequate. For these reasons, in this type of school, home-visiting and casework are best carried out by qualified, full-time caseworkers, who have experience of the special problems of handicapped children. Such caseworkers are not only indispensable members of the school team, they are also trained to give parents the understanding and support which can help to lessen tensions and anxieties at home, and so create a happier and more stable environment for the child.

In the school described here, two of the members of the School Care Committee were full-time, fully trained caseworkers from the Invalid Children's Aid Association, serving in a voluntary capacity. Many of the children were already known to them or their colleagues before their admission to school, and their observations and assessment of home conditions proved invaluable, the more so when the caseworkers concerned were invited to attend the routine medical examinations and could discuss their findings.

During the period previous to the survey, from 1957 to 1959, one of these two caseworkers was regularly present at the school medical examinations. During the survey, and subsequently, all reports on home-visiting were made from notes by the secretary of the School Care Committee who was, for the greater part of the time, a voluntary worker. With the best will in the world and despite a long record of voluntary service, it was clear that such an arrangement was of far less value to the team than direct report and discussion with the qualified social worker in actual contact with the child and his home.

A detailed account of home-visits is given later (Chapter 5), but the current problem is essentially the familiar one of a voluntary organization which, after pioneering and developing some particular aspect of social work, gradually relinquishes it to social agencies whose members are professionally trained and qualified.

THE PARENTS AS MEMBERS OF THE TEAM

The last members of the team to be considered here, though they should perhaps have been the first, are the parents. For it is the parents who bear the greatest responsibility for the day-to-day supervision and treatment of the children and for carrying out the advice given by the specialists. In the vast majority of cases parents discharge their heavy responsibilities to the best of their ability and often with great understanding, devotion and self-sacrifice.

COORDINATION

In addition to working with this team around and within the school, the school doctor has to act as liaison officer between the different hospitals and departments concerned, the Council's visiting consultants and the children's own doctors.

The school doctor is normally responsible for a number of schools and clinics and can only give a limited amount of time to each. In some schools medical sessions are regarded as interfering unduly with the educational programme. Medical inspections in the school in this survey were held about once every two or three weeks. Whenever possible, the school doctor also attended the visiting consultants' sessions held twice a term.

At the routine sessions new admissions were seen and a group of children normally submitted for their yearly medical inspection. Special problems relating to any particular child were brought forward by any member of the team and discussed, if necessary, with the class teacher and the parents. In a school for physically handicapped children, however, situations can change rapidly following an operation or other specialized treatment, and each child should be seen at least once a term.

In view of the obvious gaps in the overall supervision of the handicapped child, the role of the school doctor in coordinating all the agencies concerned is one of considerable responsibility. He should be in close contact with the hospitals with regard to treatment (physiotherapy, etc.), appliances (repair and renewal), and general medical progress. He should assist consultants by reporting on the children's progress or difficulties in school, particularly in cases of epilepsy or severe behavioural disorders. In one such case where hemispherectomy was contemplated, it was subsequently considered unnecessary following reports of the child's improvement in the school situation. Contact with the general practitioner, particularly in cases of inter-current illness or sedation, is also essential.

The primary task of the school doctor, therefore, should be to coordinate all the agencies dealing with the child: the hospitals, the visiting consultants, the general practitioner, the caseworker visiting the home, the health team in the school—physiotherapists, speech therapists, nursing Sister, teachers—and the parents.

This approach involves a detailed knowledge of each child and his environment which is difficult to achieve if there are frequent changes of medical personnel. It adds weight to the suggestion that routine examinations should take place more frequently and at least once a term. It also underlines the value of the proposal, included later in the recommendations, that there should be fortnightly or monthly case conferences in school.

The school doctor, in close cooperation with the headmistress, should arrange case conferences to discuss the problems of particular children when necessary. These could be held during the dinner hour or immediately after school and should include, in addition to the headmistress and the school doctor, the class teacher of the child concerned, the school Sister, the caseworker and the educational psychologist.

Where the child is attending a child guidance clinic, or where there are particular psychological difficulties, the psychiatrist or psychiatric social worker from the clinic should be invited to attend.

Regular case conferences, held fortnightly or monthly to discuss cases of particular interest or difficulty to any member of the team, can help towards a deeper understanding of the problems of handicapped children in general and to closer cooperation throughout the school.

CHAPTER 3

Medical Problems

THE PHYSICAL HANDICAPS: TYPES AND SEVERITY

TABLE 2 gives some details of the fifty children studied: their age and sex, the diagnosis and severity of the handicap, and any additional handicaps. It also records transfers to other schools or to home tuition during the course of the survey.

TABLE 2

The Children and their Handicaps

Case No.	Name	Age Yr. Mo.		Diagnosis	Severity of Handicap*	Additional Handicaps	School Transfers during Survey
1	Keith	11	4	Bilateral hydronephrosis	Slight (Severe)	—	Secondary day PH
2	Lionel	11	10	R. hemiplegia (traumatic)	Severe	Retardation, maladjustment	Secondary day PH
3	Malcolm	11	10	Bilateral talipes	Slight	Retardation, speech defect	Secondary day PH
4	Billy	11	4	Poliomyelitis (shoulder, arm)	Moderate	—	Secondary day PH
5	Stephen	11	0	Spastic paraplegia (athetoid)	Severe	Speech defect, aesophageal stricture, maladjustment, hearing loss (left ear)	Secondary day PH
6	Rosalind	11	9	Spastic paraplegia	Moderate	Hearing defect, speech defect	Secondary day PH

* The assessment was that given by the parents at the survey interview. The doctor's assessment is given in parenthesis in five cases in which it differed from that of the parents.

Case No.	Name	Age Yr. Mo.	Diagnosis	Severity of Handicap	Additional Handicaps	School Transfers during Survey
7	Rosemary	12 0	R. hemiplegia	Moderate	Epilepsy, retardation	Secondary day PH
8	Charlie	9 5	TB spine	Slight	—	Ordinary school
9	Hubert	8 8	Multiple congenital defects (Fallot's tetralogy, cretinism)	Severe	Speech defect, retardation	Residential PH
10	Vernon	10 2	Paraplegia (ataxic)	Moderate	—	Residential PH
11	George	7 7	Haemophilia	Severe	Poliomyelitis (R. leg)	Home tuition (out county)
12	Bertie	8 8	Fallot's tetralogy (dextrocardia)	Severe	—	—
13	Sally	10 4	Spinal tumour (intramedullary)	Slight	Maladjustment (Severe)	—
14	Robin	5 11	Cerebral tumour (thalamic glioma)	Severe	Hydrocephalus, paraplegia, retardation	—
15	Edward	9 11	Poliomyelitis (both legs)	Moderate	—	—
16	Thomas	5 2	L. hemiplegia	Slight	Epilepsy, speech defect	—
17	Monica	10 1	Paraplegia (ataxic)	Slight	Epilepsy, speech defect	—
18	Stuart	10 2	R. Hemiplegia (ectropion following angioma)	Slight	—	—
19	Mary	13 6	Multiple congenital defects (spina bifida, Fallot's tetralogy, etc.)	Severe	Speech defect, hearing defect, retardation	—
20	Edgar	10 2	Chronic osteomyelitis	Slight	Maladjustment (persistent enuresis)	—
21	Rosie	11 1	TB meningitis (ataxic paraplegia)	Moderate	Maladjustment, retardation	—
22	Doreen	7 11	Paraplegia (ataxic)	Moderate	Speech defect, retardation	—
23	Nicola	4 10	Achondroplasia	Slight	—	—
24	Susan	5 11	Sturge-Weber syndrome	Severe	Epilepsy, retardation, maladjustment	—
25	Timothy	8 0	Epilepsy	Slight	Speech defect	—
26	Brian	11 6	Paraplegia (athetoid)	Severe	Hearing defect, speech defect	Residential PH

33

Case No.	Name	Age Yr. Mo.		Diagnosis	Severity of Handicap	Additional Handicaps	School Transfers during Survey
27	Christopher	9	7	R. hemiplegia	Slight	Epilepsy, speech defect	—
28	Tessa	11	5	Paraplegia (ataxic)	Moderate	Hydrocephalus	—
29	Naomi	7	6	Poliomyelitis (R. leg)	Slight	—	Ordinary school
30	Jill	9	3	Muscular dystrophy	Severe	Speech defect, retardation, talipes	—
31	Katie	10	7	Atrial septal defect	Moderate (Severe)	Scoliosis, maladjustment	—
32	Barbara	5	6	L. hemiplegia	Moderate	Epilepsy, speech defect, asthma	—
33	Mandy	7	1	L. hemiplegia (ataxic)	Slight (Severe)	PTB, asthma	—
34	Carol	6	0	L. monoplegia	Slight	—	—
35	Eveline	7	6	Paraplegia (athetoid)	Severe	Speech defect, maladjustment	—
36	Harold	7	6	Poliomyelitis (both legs)	Severe	—	—
37	Gerald	11	2	Bilateral talipes	Slight	Retardation	—
38	Sammy	9	8	R. hemiplegia	Severe	Epilepsy, retardation	—
39	Walter	7	3	Poliomyelitis (L. leg)	Slight	—	Ordinary school
40	Oliver	7	5	Poliomyelitis (R. leg)	Slight	—	Ordinary school
41	Hughie	7	0	Fallot's tetralogy	Severe	Epilepsy, maladjustment	—
42	Terry	9	10	Haemophilia	Severe	Maladjustment	—
43	Noel	6	10	Poliomyelitis (R. leg)	Slight	—	Ordinary school
44	Ernie	7	1	Spastic paraplegia	Slight	Speech defect	—
45	Robert	7	0	Parasternal murmur (simple)	Slight	—	Ordinary school
46	John	6	1	Haemophilia	Severe	—	—
47	Chris	6	9	Muscular dystrophy	Moderate (Severe)	Maladjustment	—
48	Francis	9	2	Epispadias	Severe	—	—
49	Quintin	8	2	Haemophilia	Severe	Maladjustment	Day open-air school
50	Edwin	7	8	Poliomyelitis (R. leg)	Moderate	—	—

The 'severity of the handicap' was the assessment given by the parents during the interview. These assessments were confirmed by the doctor in all but five cases (where the doctor's assessment is shown in parenthesis). The discrepancies are an interesting reflection of the parents' attitudes. In two instances (Case 1, a boy with bilateral hydro-nephrosis, and Case 13, a girl with an intramedullary spinal tumour) the doctor's assessment was 'severe' in view of the diagnosis, and the parents' 'slight'. In both cases the mothers appeared unable to accept the grave outlook. In Case 47, a boy with progressive muscular dystrophy (whose younger brother had recently been found to have the same condition), the mother described the handicap as 'moderate', but she added 'at present'. In the other two cases (31 and 33), the mothers' inability to recognize the seriousness of their children's conditions appeared to arise, on the one hand, from a general attitude of guilt and rejection and, on the other, from an unwillingness to acknowledge her severe limitations in both physical and mental development. The types of handicap and the numbers of cases of each are shown in Table 3.

TABLE 3
The Types of Handicap

Type of handicap	No. of cases
Cerebral palsy (neo-natal)	14
Cerebral palsy (secondary)	7
Poliomyelitis	8
Congenital cardiac defects	4
Haemophilia	4
Muscular dystrophy	2
Multiple congenital defects	2
Bilateral talipes equino varus	2
Epispadias	1
Urethral stricture (with bilateral hydronephrosis)	1
TB spine	1
Chronic osteomyelitis of femur	1
Achondroplasia	1
Epilepsy	1
Spinal tumour (intramedullary)	1
Total	50

In some cases categories overlap. For example, in addition to the four children under the heading of 'congenital cardiac defects' there were two with Fallot's tetralogy who appear under the heading of 'multiple congenital defects'.

Two of the four cases of congenital heart defects also had Fallot's tetralogy and one was an atrial septal defect. The fourth was the child whose original diagnosis of ventricular septal defect was revised at seven years, and who was no longer considered handicapped.

The seven cases of cerebral palsy secondary to other conditions were: (i) spastic paraplegia resulting from cerebral tumour (thalamic glioma) at twenty months; (ii) spastic paraplegia resulting from TB meningitis at eight and a half months; (iii) spastic paraplegia resulting from depressed fracture of the skull at four years eight months; and (iv) spastic hemiplegia resulting from an extensive haemangioma of head and face, and cerebral haemorrhage at four months. There is less certainty about the other three cases that are included in this category, where the evidence is from the medical history as given by the mother; (v) spastic paraplegia following severe gastro-enteritis, possibly complicated by thrombophlebitis, at four months; (vi) left hemiplegia following severe convulsions in a fever hospital at ten and a half months; (vii) left hemiplegia following severe whooping cough at ten months.

The twenty-one cases of cerebral palsy are listed by type in Table 4.

TABLE 4
Cerebral Palsy Cases

Type of cerebral palsy	No. of cases
Spastic monoplegia	1
Spastic hemiplegia	9
Spastic tetraplegia	1
Spastic paraplegia	3
Ataxic paraplegia	4
Athetoid paraplegia	3
Total	21

CONGENITAL HANDICAPS: SPECIAL PROBLEMS

The emotional problems of children with congenital handicaps differ in many respects from those whose handicaps are acquired. Thirty-one of the fifty children in the survey had congenital or neo-natal handicaps. Emotional problems appeared particularly difficult in the five cases of confirmed congenital cardiac defects, in part perhaps due to their severity, or to their association with multiple handicaps, but mainly because of the poor prognosis. The combination of a congenital cardiac defect with a poor prognosis appeared to give rise to the most intractable emotional problems.

Of the five cases of severe congenital cardiac defect (9, 12, 19, 41 and 31) the first four had undergone a Blalock operation. In these cases, however, there was still some evidence of heart failure, and the prognosis was poor because transposition of the great vessels made further operation too hazardous. In each instance the parents had the utmost difficulty in accepting the prognosis.

Two of the five (31 and 41) were maladjusted and referred for child guidance. Their cases will be discussed more fully in Chapter 10 with the other cases in which child guidance was recommended.

ACQUIRED HANDICAPS

The Poliomyelitis Cases

The children with paralysis following poliomyelitis formed the largest single group and their handicaps were slight or moderately severe in degree. In fact, four of them were able to return to ordinary school during the period of the survey. The parents were able to accept this type of handicap more easily, perhaps because they did not feel themselves responsible. Seven of the children, too—all with paralysis of the lower limbs—seemed to have accepted their handicaps and to be coping with their difficulties reasonably well. In the one case involving the upper limbs, the child—who had a flail right arm—appeared to find it much harder to adjust himself and tended to be rather depressed and withdrawn.

The numbers of children with paralytic poliomyelitis are now falling rapidly following immunization campaigns and cases are already becoming increasingly rare, at least in primary schools for the physically handicapped.

The Cerebral Palsy Cases

The group of seven children with *acquired* cerebral palsy presented much greater problems than the neo-natal palsies or the children with paralytic poliomyelitis. Indeed, this type of handicap appeared to be among the most difficult for both parents and children to accept.

Lionel (Case 2) had fallen twenty feet through the glass roof of a garage when he was four and a half years old. He had sustained a depressed fracture and had been unconscious for twenty-one days and in hospital for five months. He was left with a severe right hemiplegia, retardation and, subsequently, maladjustment.

There was evidence of difficulties in this family before the accident, since an older brother had attended the Institute for Child Psychology. The strain was clearly increased by Lionel's condition and by the fact that the family was not accepted for emigration to Australia on his account. The grandparents—they were to have accompanied the family— were the most disappointed and showed their resentment towards the child. Lionel had great difficulty in adjusting to his handicap and always spoke of his 'poor arm'. He appeared to feel himself rejected at home and became sexually precocious and difficult to manage in school. During the questionnaire interview and in the course of discussing his problems, his mother, who had previously proved rather uncooperative, asked if Lionel might be referred for child guidance to the same Institute that his brother had previously attended with good results.

Stephen (Case 5) developed gastro-enteritis at four months, which was later thought to have been complicated by thrombo-phlebitis, leaving him with a severe athetoid paraplegia. He could neither stand unsupported nor walk, and his speech was almost unintelligible. His father had remained convinced, in spite of all explanations, that the reason for his sudden relapse in hospital was that he had been dropped. Although both parents were devoted to the child, marital relations deteriorated from this time, and the father took a job on permanent night-shift. Eventually, the parents were barely on speaking terms, although they both continued to make every effort to help their handicapped child.

With all the families concerned, regular casework was undertaken by trained caseworkers from the Invalid Children's Aid Association *when the children reached school* and considerable improvements were achieved in most instances. The time when such casework was most needed and could have been most effective, however, was undoubtedly when the handicap was first recognized.

ADDITIONAL HANDICAPS

Twenty-nine (58 per cent) of the children had additional handicaps, as shown in Table 5.

TABLE 5
Additional Handicaps

Handicap	No. of cases	
Severe hearing loss	3	(2)*
Speech defects	15	(10)
Mental retardation	11	(3)
Maladjustment (referred to child guidance unit)	12	(2)
Epilepsy	8	(6)
Visual defects	6	(2)

* The figures in parentheses indicate the numbers of children whose main handicap was cerebral palsy.

Speech or hearing defects, in particular, tended to add considerably to the isolation and frustration of the children and speech therapy was of great importance in their rehabilitation.

DUAL HANDICAPS: PHYSICAL AND MENTAL

Six children were suffering from 'dual defects', i.e. they were both physically and mentally handicapped. If the physical handicap had not been given preference, they would probably have been deemed educationally subnormal or ineducable, and would have attended a school for the educationally subnormal or a training centre. Two children with multiple congenital defects, three with cerebral palsy, and one with a bilateral talipes came within this category. Where there are dual defects the physical defect normally takes precedence, and it is often difficult to make an accurate assessment of educational ability in a handicapped child of pre-school age.

ASSESSMENT OF EDUCATIONAL ABILITY

Because of the problems it presents, assessment of intellectual ability in a handicapped child is best done by an educational psychologist with a special interest in such children. A child may score on a standardized test at a low or even feeble-minded level, not because he lacks intelligence but because he lacks the normal communication skills on which performance of the tests depends.

An additional complication stems from the fact that the parents of physically handicapped children tend to be especially sensitive about sending them to a 'silly' school, i.e. one where the children are mentally handicapped. Parents with children who are both physically and mentally handicapped often find it easier to accept the physical handicap and to regard the mental handicap as arising from it.

In any case, the whole question of intelligence quotients is a sensitive one for the people involved—parents and educationists, teachers and even politicians. The reliability of IQ tests has been called in question, and there has been much discussion of the variations apparent in relation to whether the tests are carried out in familiar circumstances or not, the methods of approach by different examiners, and the periods for which such measurements are valid.

It was therefore agreed, for the purposes of this survey, to make 'a graded assessment of each pupil's ability to deal with the problems presented by day-to-day living, in view of his physical, or physical and mental, handicap'. This assessment was made jointly by the headmistress, the educational psychologist attached to the school, and the school doctor, with the results shown in Table 6. The figures follow the general pattern of distribution of ability in normal schools at a slightly lower level of attainment, an encouraging finding in view of the various difficulties discussed above.

TABLE 6

Assessment of Educational Ability

Assessment	No. of children
Much below average ability	6*
Below average ability	16
Of average ability	19
Above average ability	9

* The six children with dual defects.

THE MEDICAL SUPERVISION OF THE HANDICAPPED CHILD

It is in the overall medical supervision of the handicapped child that the most serious shortcomings are found: there is a wide gap between what is needed and what is achieved.

Apley and MacKeith (1962) state in their foreword: 'In illness the whole person is involved . . . it is logical to look at the whole person, body and mind. This is the comprehensive, psycho-somatic approach. It is needed not only in psycho-somatic disorders, but in *all* illness, whether common or rare, acute or chronic, trivial or lethal . . . Many disorders cannot be understood unless, with the physical aspects, the intellectual, emotional and social aspects of the patient are considered. For detailed study the doctor may take the patient to pieces; but to understand the person who is ill, the doctor must put him together again.'

Experience in the survey suggests that pieces of the handicapped child may be satisfactorily treated in hospital—a limb, or a heart, or whatever is involved—but that little consideration is given as to who is to put *all* the pieces together again. Who is to take the responsibility for considering not only the physical aspects of the child but also his 'intellectual, emotional and social aspects' and, furthermore, those of his family?

The pattern of medical supervision revealed in the survey was repeated over and over again. Apart from hospital admissions for diagnosis or treatment, it consisted of visits to hospital, usually at intervals of six months (but varying from three to twelve months), and an annual medical inspection by the school doctor. In addition, the children with cardiac, orthopaedic, or cerebral palsy defects were seen by the Council's visiting consultants two or three times a year for their specific defects. Special examinations for other conditions, such as poor nutrition, intercurrent infections, or behaviour problems took place if requested by the school Sister, the teaching staff, or the parents. In only one case, that of the boy with epispadias, was a child seen by his own general practitioner, *on account of his handicap*, at fairly regular intervals. In the other forty-nine cases, the parents stated quite categorically that their children were seen by their general practitioners only on the occurrence of special, i.e. unrelated, illness. Once a child has been referred to hospital for his handicap —by his own doctor, a welfare clinic, or the obstetric unit—it appears that the responsibility for him as a whole person, body and mind, including the physical, intellectual, emotional, and social aspects of his case, has been handed over to that hospital—yet clearly few, if any, hospitals can fulfil these responsibilities.

Handicap

It is possible that within the hospital itself, and with the cooperation of social workers, almoners, the psychiatric department if called upon, and others, the supervision of the whole child may be achieved. But once the child has been discharged, overall supervision is liable to vanish like a pipe-dream. The six-monthly visits to hospital outpatient departments are often largely routine and mainly, if not exclusively, concerned with the physical handicap or with the supervision of appliances. They are often carried out by junior members of the staff who change frequently and have little or no previous knowledge of the children concerned. It is hardly possible in a busy outpatient department to scan through the pile of observations, reports, and recommendations on each child, or to pick out the essential problems, especially if the case is new to the examining doctor. All too frequently the mother is told: 'He's coming on nicely, Mother, bring him again in six months.' She may have had a long journey, an even longer wait in hospital, and been obliged to pay for other children to be looked after; yet when she sees the doctor, she may not even have time to gather her courage and ask the questions she had in mind. Small wonder that some appointments are missed!

Where the general practitioner has not undertaken the overall supervision of the child, as in 98 per cent of the cases in the survey, the responsibility falls on the school doctor. Yet it is clear that no real attempt can be made to fulfil such responsibility if the child is examined only once a year.

HOSPITAL ADMISSIONS

The emotional reactions that may follow the hospitalization of young children are now more generally recognized (as a result of the work of the Tavistock Clinic and particularly of James Robertson (1958)). For anyone who has seen the film 'A Two-year-old Goes to Hospital', which reveals so dramatically the grief, despair and anger of the very normal small girl who is admitted for a slight operation, it will not be difficult to imagine the effect of the prolonged or repeated admissions to hospital that the handicapped child is likely to experience.

Three of the children in the survey had been admitted to hospital twenty-two, twenty-six and thirty times, respectively, and five others between eleven and sixteen times. In some cases, no doubt, familiarity may breed, if not contempt, at least acceptance; but not in all. Usually, admissions are accompanied by painful episodes, operations, and injections or incisions, as in the case of Edgar, the child with chronic osteomyelitis and recurrent abscesses (twenty-six admissions): or by tension and anxiety, as in the numerous admissions of haemophilic children for bleeding which cannot be controlled.

A child's reaction to frequent admissions to hospital will obviously be affected by the distance of the hospital from the home, by whether visiting is easy or difficult for the family, and whether it is limited or unrestricted. Table 7 shows the frequencies with which the children were admitted to hospital, their age on admission and the duration of hospitalization.

TABLE 7
Frequency of Hospital Admission

No. of cases	Age on admission	Number of admissions						Duration wks
		None	1–2	3–5	6–10	11–19	20 and over	
1	–	1	–	–	–	–	–	0
1	A	–	1	–	–	–	–	5
2	A, B	–	1	–	–	1	–	3
6	A, C	–	2	1	3	–	–	201
5	A, B, C	–	–	1	2	2	–	117
1	B	–	1	–	–	–	–	2
19	B, C	–	8	5	2	2	2	725
15	C	–	9	3	2	–	1	512
50	Total	1	22	10	9	5	3	1,565

A = under 6 months; B = 6 months to 3 years; C = 4 years and over.

The number of admissions varied from none in one case (the little girl with achondroplasia) to over thirty for a boy with severe haemophilia. For the whole sample, the average number of admissions to hospital per child was 5·5.

The duration of the admissions ranged from one night to four years. Rosie (Case 21), the child with TB meningitis and spastic quadriplegia, following her first admission for a period of ten months when eight and a half months old, was admitted on twenty subsequent occasions for one night. Charlie (Case 8), the boy with a tuberculous spine, was admitted at three years and remained in hospital for four years until his family was rehoused. The average length of time spent in hospital for the forty-nine children admitted was thirty-two weeks.

The ages at which they were admitted varied. Thirty-three were admitted to hospital between six months and three years; thirteen were admitted before they were six months old.

The problems for the family of a handicapped child in attending hospital for supervision, treatment or visiting are considered in Chapter 5. It is difficult or impossible to separate the emotional complications arising from prolonged or repeated hospitalization from all the other difficulties of handicapped children, but it is an inescapable fact that this factor in itself can constitute a major problem of adjustment for the handicapped child.

THE PARENTS' PROBLEMS

When Should Parents be Told of the Handicap?

There is not only a diversity of views on this point but a diversity of practice, both in hospitals and among family doctors, and there appears to be no generally accepted policy. A number of questions relating to this issue were therefore included in the survey questionnaire.

Parents' responses to Question 132, asking when they thought a doctor should tell the mother, were as follows:

	Responses
As soon as he suspects physical or mental defects	47
As soon as he is sure that the child is handicapped	2
Leave it to her to find out for herself	1

Thus the overwhelming majority of mothers preferred the doctor to tell them 'as soon as he suspects physical or mental defects'. Some of them expressed the point of view that as parents they felt they had the right and the responsibility to know as much as possible from the beginning.

The one mother who thought it best to 'leave it to her to find out for herself' had, in fact, been left to do so. She said that she was 'never told, but found out through the physiotherapist'. 'Glad I wasn't told—might have been too much of a shock.' This mother was herself a chronic asthmatic and suffered from anxiety and tension.

These responses, although striking, were clearly given with reference to suspicions of mental or physical defects which were subsequently confirmed. The doctor himself must obviously decide the stage at which his suspicions are sufficiently well founded to communicate them to the parents. It is equally clear that the great majority of parents wish to know of a child's handicap from the earliest possible moment.

What to Tell the Parents

The difficulties of deciding when to tell the parents are matched only by the difficulties of how much to tell them. Clearly, the information should be given over a period of time and in a number of interviews. Parents, especially young mothers with a new-born baby, are often so overwhelmed by the first suggestion of any departure from the normal that they do not hear or cannot take in anything else that is said at the time. If the specialist himself gives the initial information it may not be possible for him to give the further interviews which would enable the parents to formulate their own questions.

The question about 'when' the doctor should tell was therefore followed by a question asking the parents what had happened in their particular case:

32 mothers (64 per cent) indicated satisfaction with the way in which they were told;

11 mothers (22 per cent) complained of delay, either in diagnosis or in being told;

7 mothers (14 per cent) criticized the way in which they were told.

Of the eleven mothers who complained of delay, eight had children with cerebral palsy. Their further comments are summarized in Table 8.

TABLE 8

Delays in Establishing Diagnosis

Case No.	Child's Condition	Delay (according to parents)	Comments
6	Cerebral palsy	$3\frac{1}{2}$ years	'She's just born lazy.' (hospital)
28	Cerebral palsy	1 year	'She's just a lazy baby.' (hospital)
10	Cerebral palsy	4 years	'He will just grow out of it.' (hospital; own Dr; clinic)
34	Cerebral palsy	1 year	'She will just grow out of it.' (hospital)
18	Cerebral palsy	6 months	Delay due to loss of papers in transfer to nearer hospital
27	Cerebral palsy	Few weeks	Delay in letter to hospital from clinic
5	Cerebral palsy	18 months	'Not told soon enough.' (mother) 'Diagnosis presented many difficulties.' (hospital)
22	Cerebral palsy	1 year	Attended orthopaedic clinic for a year, but 'not told anything'. (mother)
40	Poliomyelitis	5 days	Delay in diagnosis
47	Muscular dystrophy	2 years	'Unable to discuss condition with specialist for over two years.' (mother) Mother may have failed to understand explanations given earlier by house physician.
1	Urethral stricture and bilateral hydro-nephrosis	$5\frac{1}{2}$ years	Urethral stricture was diagnosed at an early stage, but the child was transferred from general hospital to fever hospital and there was no liaison or follow-up.

In the last case in Table 8, the child had been admitted at four weeks of age to a general hospital for investigation of 'weakness and kidney trouble'. The mother was told that one kidney was infected and the baby was given injections. He developed broncho-pneumonia and was in the hospital for three months. Typhoid broke out in the ward and the baby was transferred to the fever hospital as a contact. After three weeks the mother was told, 'He is now fit and can be discharged.' On looking back, she thought that this remark may perhaps have referred only to the broncho-pneumonia, and that the fever hospital may not even have known of the kidney trouble. In any case, she had been told at the general hospital that the child would be discharged in a few weeks and therefore understood the hospital to mean that the child was cured.

There was no official follow-up, but the mother reported back to the Sister in the general hospital of her own accord when the baby was six months old. Sister agreed that the kidney condition must have cleared up, otherwise the child would not have been discharged. However, dribbling incontinence was noticed by the mother at two years, and she consulted her own doctor and the welfare clinic. She explained at the survey interview that she was repeatedly told that the child 'would grow out of it', and insisted that at no time was the urine examined.

Finally, when the child was six years old, she asked her own doctor for a letter to the hospital because of his frequent colds and coughs, and it was only then that the kidney condition was rediscovered. The changeover of hospitals and the lack of liaison and follow-up in the outcome proved disastrous, because the child developed a bilateral hydronephrosis. When asked if she had ever wanted more specialist advice, the mother replied that she had been discouraged from asking further questions, since she was 'put off' so long when she felt it was serious. If other parents came to her for advice (Question 155), however, she would tell them from her own experience: 'Go to your own doctor at once, and insist on seeing a specialist if necessary—as soon as possible'.

What Not to Tell the Parents

Deciding what not to tell the parents may be equally important, as is illustrated in the responses of seven parents who were critical of the way in which they had been told. Details of one of these cases has already been given (p.16).

In two similar cases, both severe spastics, the mothers were told in hospital after their confinement, in one case that the child would be 'blind and defective'; in the other that the child would 'neither see nor hear nor move off his back'. The first child has normal vision, is making good progress at school, and is considered to be of above average intelligence. The second child, although severely retarded, attends school, is walking and is able to take part, in his rather limited way, in the life of the school.

In these examples the attempt to avoid deception and to prepare the parents for the worst, while not so disastrous for the children, caused not only unnecessary suffering to the parents but a considerable delay in their efforts to provide the special consideration and training their children needed to help them to overcome their handicaps.

Specialist Supervision

The remaining questions in this group were intended to give some indication of how far the first and subsequent interviews with the specialist or the hospital authorities met the needs of the parents.

Question 134 asked: 'When the parents were first told, were they able to discuss with the doctor what exactly the diagnosis meant, and what the child would be like, and where they could go for advice?' Twenty-nine mothers, or 58 per cent, answered 'No'; seven mothers added that they had been able to discuss these aspects later, but with the ward Sister or the physiotherapist, not the doctor.

What happened to the parents in Case 22 is, unfortunately, not so rare an occurrence. Doreen was a first baby, her mother was found to have severe toxaemia, and she was born by Caesarean section at seven months, weighing 2·15 lb. She was kept in an incubator until eight weeks and allowed home at three months, weighing 5·7 lb. Subsequently, the mother noticed that the baby was slow in sitting, crawling and walking. She attended her own doctor and was referred to the orthopaedic department of a children's hospital, when the baby was two and a half years old.

The mother was told to bring the child back every three months for observation for about a year, but was told nothing more. Eventually, the father got time off work, attended hospital with the mother, and took the opportunity of looking at the casebook over the nurse's shoulder, where he saw the word 'spastic'. He had no idea what it meant, but persisted in his requests for information. After this interview the child was transferred to the cerebral palsy unit.

It is perhaps only fair to add that the mother was a very nervous woman who had had two thyroid operations, the second three months after the conception of this child. She observed that she had always wondered about the cause of the child's handicap: 'Was it something to do with the operation?'

'At Risk' Registers

It is of interest to note, in relation to some of the children's histories, particularly those of the cerebral palsy cases, that had the scheme of 'at risk' registers now in use in maternity and child welfare clinics and obstetric hospitals been in operation when these children were infants, 50 per cent of them would have appeared on 'at risk' cards for close supervision. The proportion is considerably higher if the nineteen cases where the handicap was acquired are excluded. Twenty-five (about 77 per cent) of the thirty-one cases of congenital or neo-natal handicaps, if they had attended a clinic operating an 'at risk' register, would have been followed up at frequent intervals because of a history of antenatal haemorrhage, prolonged labour, abnormal delivery, the Rhesus factor, anoxaemia, or the presence of a recognizable abnormality. Of the 10 per cent who were Rhesus-negative, it is probable that, with the knowledge now available, the ensuing handicaps might have been less severe or even prevented altogether.

Question 135 dealt with opportunities for discussing the 'placement' of the child, interpreted in the interview as 'school placement' rather than placement in an institution, which did not appear to be envisaged by most parents. The great majority of the parents answered that they were able to discuss this question satisfactorily and had time for consideration.

Question 136 asked: 'Have the parents ever wanted more specialist advice than has been given?' Eighteen mothers answered that they had wanted more specialist advice before the diagnosis was made and sixteen others had wanted more advice after the diagnosis was established. Eight mothers had wanted more advice both before and after they knew what the child was suffering from. Satisfaction with the amount of specialist advice received was expressed by 48 per cent of the mothers.

Finally, in answer to an open question (Question 141): 'Is there any way in which the authorities could make things easier for the parents of handicapped children?', eight mothers (16 per cent) said that they wished they could have occasional interviews with the specialist to discuss the handling of the child and his problems.

This point was well illustrated by Case 21, the child who had tuberculous meningitis at five and a half months. After nine months in hospital, Rosie was sent for convalescence for three weeks. Immediately on her return from the convalescent home, when eighteen months old, she was sent home without any particular instructions and the parents felt quite helpless as to what to do or how to handle her, especially since she was their first baby. They had received no special advice except that she was to attend hospital weekly for X-rays and lumbar punctures.

There is clearly much room for improvement with regard to communication between medical personnel and the parents of handicapped children, when 58 per cent of the parents stated that, when they were first told about their child's handicap, they had been unable to discuss it with the doctor concerned and had not been informed how and where they could get further advice; and when 52 per cent reported that they would have liked more specialist help than they had received in caring for their child thereafter.

The need for advice and guidance that was expressed by these mothers referred primarily to the handling of the physical problems of their children. In addition, one or two of the parents were able to ask for help with the emotional problems involved. In subsequent chapters it will be seen that these problems existed to no less an extent than in the health department referred to by Caplan (1961). This department was dealing with a thousand new cases a year of children with disabling physical handicaps, 'all of whom have some form of emotional complications, and many of whom have explicit psychiatric symptomatology'. To paraphrase the same author, a baby with a congenital abnormality creates a situation which requires immediate and specialized attention, particularly during the critical period of the first two months after birth when the mother has first to face herself, and then her family and the community, with what she feels is her own imperfect creation: 'How much time and wasted professional energy would be saved, not to mention avoidable unhappiness and personality distortions for family and child, if community leaders were to realize [this]'.

There will, moreover, be many other critical periods during the child's development when the parents and especially the mother will need urgent and expert guidance if 'avoidable unhappiness and personality distortions' are to be prevented. She will be greatly helped if there is some continuity of supervision—if she knows someone to whom she can turn, someone who is already familiar with, and understands, her particular situation and problems.

For these reasons, I suggest that, whenever a congenital abnormality or severe handicap is diagnosed in a baby, the mother should be seen as soon as possible, and certainly before she leaves the hospital, by a psychiatric social worker, or an almoner with some knowledge in this field, so that arrangements can be made to follow her up in her own home directly she is discharged. The most effective follow-up would be regular supervision in the home by a trained caseworker attached to an agency (such as the Invalid Children's Aid Association) which specializes in this type of work. Subsequently, when the child is old enough, an educational psychologist should, if necessary, be called in to assess his educational potential and needs.

The question of what kinds of agency are available, and what is required of them, inevitably arises. Clearly, the best service would be provided by full-time caseworkers trained in this particular field and supervised by a consultant psychiatric social worker with relevant experience. The caseworkers should be able to deal with any mental health problems as they arise, as well as with the social problems that the presence of a handicapped child creates for the family. Hence there must be opportunities for in-service training and for consultation about especially difficult cases. In this survey the Invalid Children's Aid Association for the most part met these requirements, but its caseworkers are not available outside London and the Home Counties. The Association is, moreover, subject to all the limitations and pressures that are experienced by an organization dependent on voluntary contributions.

It has been suggested that this type of supervision might be undertaken in each area by a number of specially trained Health Visitors or members of mental health departments; or that child guidance workers with a special interest in this field might be allocated to it. Such proposals would involve considerable changes in policy and long-term planning.

In London, meanwhile, it should be possible to make greater use of the Invalid Children's Aid Association which, in general, goes far to meet the needs of handicapped children and their parents.

If similar facilities could be developed by local authorities for the handicapped children and their families in their own areas, a new and valuable contribution to community mental health could be achieved.

CHAPTER 4

Educational Problems

THERE are many ways in which a physical handicap can also constitute a serious educational disability.

The initial illness or operation, and the time spent in hospital, can have emotional and educational consequences as well as physical. Adjustment to the handicap itself needs the child's concentration, time and energy, and he may be required to adjust to a new school as well.

He may lose time from school for visits to hospital for supervision or treatment. Physiotherapy, occupational therapy and speech therapy, whether in hospital or school, all mean loss of time and loss of continuity in the child's education. Treatment periods also present difficulties for the teacher in a class of handicapped children, because different children may be absent from class at different times all through the week.

School attendance is affected not only by hospital admissions and other treatments, but often by ill health, fatigue or the after-effects of therapy. Similarly, handicapped children frequently suffer from inability to concentrate through anxiety, fatigue or ill health, and sometimes through brain damage. Their powers of communication may be severely limited as a result of speech or hearing defects and their manual skills may be impaired by paralysis or by inability to coordinate muscular effort.

It is evident that teachers in schools for handicapped children should be carefully selected and trained. Not only must they have unlimited patience, but they need specialized training to enable them to understand the emotional and perceptual problems of handicapped children and to apply appropriate teaching methods for widely different types of disability.

LOSS OF SCHOOL TIME

Hospitalization

The psychological effects of repeated or prolonged admissions to hospital are considered in Chapter 7. Here we are concerned with the consequences of hospital admissions on the child's education.

The amount of time lost and the ages at which it was lost varied greatly (see Table 7). As noted in the previous chapter, the average number of admissions to hospital per child was five and a half and the average length of time spent in hospital was thirty-two weeks. Although long-stay cases may receive some hospital tuition, long periods of absence from school must constitute an educational handicap.

Associated Illness and Debility

The following cases illustrate loss of school time for reasons other than hospitalization.

Mandy (Case 33), a frail child, developed various chest complications after the severe whooping cough and pneumonia which were thought to have led to her spastic hemiplegia. Following bronchitis, a collapsed lower lobe and bronchiectasis, she developed pulmonary tuberculosis. She was more absent than present in school and hardly able to take any active part in lessons even when present. Her family of five lived in two small rooms on a top floor; they had a stove on the landing and shared an outside lavatory with ten other tenants. The family was subsequently rehoused and since the termination of the survey the child has been admitted to a day open-air school where she is improving.

The children with epilepsy (of whom there were nine) also tended to lose a good deal of time from school, during and after their fits. In one case this was the main handicap, but in the other eight it was an additional complication.

School attendances have been checked for each child, where possible for three terms, to give an overall picture of the rate of absence. The percentage of possible attendances was 81·7, indicating about 20 per cent absenteeism. This is approximately twice the rate for children in ordinary schools.

Supervision and Treatment

Handicapped children are frequently interrupted in their school work because it is necessary for them to have special treatment or supervision. The loss of school time has been greatly reduced since facilities for physiotherapy, occupational therapy and speech therapy have been introduced into schools.

Handicap

In the sample studied, the following numbers of children were receiving such treatment either in school, or at hospital, and in two cases at school during the term, and at hospital during the holiday.

	No. of children
Physiotherapy (school only)	18
Physiotherapy (hospital only)	9
Physiotherapy (school and hospital)	2
Occupational therapy (school only)	9
Speech therapy (school only)	11

The nine children who had physiotherapy at hospital were all under one of the physical medicine departments at a children's hospital where the Bobath method for the treatment of cerebral palsy is practised and their parents had wished them to continue with this method.

School hours lost weekly through treatment at school varied from fifteen minutes for a mild speech defect to four hours for a severe cerebral palsy requiring physiotherapy and occupational and speech therapy. The children who attended hospital lost a total of between two and five hours a week for one or two half-hour treatments, depending on the time taken up in travelling and in waiting for treatment. Therefore, whenever possible, such treatment was arranged out of school hours or at the beginning or end of a school session.

LOSS OF EDUCATIONAL SKILLS

More specifically educational problems associated with handicapped children include the loss or impairment of communication through speech or hearing, the loss of manual skills, and emotional retardation attributable to the handicap and its treatment.

Impaired Communication

Twelve children (24 per cent) had marked speech defects, for which speech therapy was required. The therapy was given at school during term time and two children continued it at hospital during the holidays.

In seven of these cases (six with cerebral palsies, and one with multiple congenital defects), speech was so severely affected that normal communication was extremely difficult. Three of the cases were associated with severe hearing loss, but the main difficulty in all seven was dysarthria associated with the cerebral palsy.

Eveline (Case 35), whose intelligence was above average in spite of severe spastic paraplegia and athetosis, had so marked a speech defect that even her mother was frequently unable to understand her. This, in conjunction with her severe general incapacity (she was unable to stand or walk) and her emotional problems, produced so much frustration that she had almost daily severe temper tantrums lasting up to an hour at a time. Her tantrums became much less frequent and distressing when she was admitted to school, where the regular speech therapy she received enabled her to make herself better understood.

Brian (Case 26), a child with a similar severe athetoid paraplegia and marked speech and hearing loss, was transferred to the deaf unit recently established at a residential school for handicapped children, for intensive auditory and speech training.

Loss of Muscular Coordination and Manual Skills

Loss of muscular coordination and spatial perception can constitute a major difficulty in the education of the handicapped child. The loss of a limb through congenital malformation, amputation, or paralysis is a severe handicap, but it is limited and predictable. The loss of muscular coordination in the spastic and the involuntary movements of the athetoid child may have unlimited and unpredictable effects, which frequently become worse the greater the efforts made to control them. The spastic child must learn to relax and inhibit before he can achieve purposeful movements successfully. The paralysis is seldom confined to one limb and may affect his whole body. Therapy is aimed at helping these children to learn methods whereby they can improve control of these purposeless movements. For example, Brian (Case 26) frequently held his head between his hands to prevent excessive movement when he was trying to talk and make himself understood.

The acquisition of educational and social skills is obviously a very complex task with this type of handicap. Furthermore, since the initial paralysis is due to brain damage, the child's intellectual capacity may also be impaired. These problems were most commonly seen in the children with cerebral palsy (42 per cent), fourteen with cerebral palsy of congenital or neo-natal origin and seven with cerebral palsy secondary to other conditions.

Loss of Development-stimulating Experiences

Handicapped children suffer yet another disability in that they are deprived of early development-stimulating experiences. For example Brian (Case 26), whose parents were told when he was three days old that he might be mentally defective, blind, deaf, or all three, was considered grossly defective until he was a year old. The mother, a capable, intelligent, and affectionate woman whose skill and cooperation with physicians, physiotherapists and speech therapists have since enabled the child to make full use of his more than average ability, was discouraged from making any attempt to stimulate or assist his hearing, speech, or development during the crucial first year of life.

In two other cases (35 and 38) the parents believed their children to be mentally defective in their infancy and as a result these children were deprived of many important early experiences.

Cerebral palsy in particular precludes children, to a greater or lesser degree, from participating in a normal range of childhood experiences. Their inability to go shopping, help with the cooking, or to play normally with other children puts them at a disadvantage, which is often compounded by defects of speech or hearing which prevent them from asking the questions by which a child extends his knowledge of the world around him.

EMOTIONAL RETARDATION

Handicapped children may become emotionally retarded through the stresses involved in adjusting to their handicap. In particular, children whose handicaps are acquired may be almost overwhelmed for a time by their inability to continue to take part in activities they previously enjoyed, such as football and other sports and the everyday rough-and-tumble with their friends. This was the case, for example, with the eight children who had paralysis following poliomyelitis.

Billy (Case 4), a child of eleven with a flail right arm, attended hospital every three or four months for a new arm and shoulder splint. He said constantly to his mother: 'If only I had both arms.' She described him as sensitive and highly strung: 'Reads all the time, and won't go out to play. He's too quiet.' The teacher's comment was: 'Timid, somewhat anxious, shy and withdrawn.'

Edward (Case 15), a boy with two paralysed lower limbs (one slightly, the other severely), found great difficulty in settling down in a school for the physically handicapped. 'He hated it at first', 'seeing children who were worse', and truanted frequently; 'now he's used to it'.

Noel (Case 43), a boy with partial paralysis of the right leg, asked his mother: 'Why do I have sticks (crutches) when Eileen (his sister) doesn't?' Edwin (Case 50), another boy in this category, frequently asked his mother: 'Will my leg ever be better? Will I be able to run like the other boys?' She added: 'He gets moody and irritable.'

These children's obvious pre-occupation with their disabilities would inhibit their capacity to learn and thus result in varying degrees of emotional retardation.

The handicapped child's natural resentment may be increased when he sees younger brothers and sisters outstrip him. Wise parents can help him to face such difficulties, but over-anxiety may increase them, and over-protection will tend to sap his independence.

Hardest of all for the handicapped child is a situation in which, for external reasons such as financial stress in a large family, difficult or over-crowded housing conditions, or a refusal of emigration permits on account of the handicap, he feels rejected by his parents or siblings. In such cases the child has little heart for educational effort, especially if he can see no prospects that will not be marred by his handicap.

SCHOOL LIFE AND THE HANDICAPPED CHILD

The general effect of school life on the handicapped child appears out-standingly good. The child who has been isolated by his disability, at home or in hospital, usually responds quickly to the companionship of other children equally handicapped.

Absorption in new interests and especially in normal activities when-ever possible, such as physical education and swimming, gives the child renewed energy and confidence. School discipline can give a child a sense of security and normality which is especially valuable if the parents have been over-anxious or over-protective. It is perhaps surprising to see how often skilled and sympathetic handling of the children by their teachers brings about not only social and educational achievements, but remark-able physical improvement.

When Susan (Case 24) arrived in school, a child with an extensive haemangioma of face, neck and shoulder, and hemiplegia following cerebral haemorrhage at four months associated with fits, her temper tantrums were so severe that the hospital was considering hemispherectomy. She came from very poor social conditions. Her methods of communication were largely spitting, swearing and constant aggression. The possibility of sending her to a residential school was carefully examined at the request of the headmistress, but it was finally agreed that she was too young and she remained at the day school.

Close contact was maintained with the hospital, and school reports were sent when the child's hospital appointments were due. In view of her improvement, the proposed operation was postponed. After she had been in school about eighteen months, no further reference was made to the need for operation. The child had become, through the continuous efforts and boundless patience of the teaching staff, an accepted and useful member of her class and of the school. At home her aggression was still a serious problem and she sometimes had lapses of behaviour and language in school, usually heralding a fit. She was acutely aware of her gross disfigurement but had managed to discuss even this with the headmistress, confiding in her her hopes that one day 'Jesus won't be quite so busy and he may be able to hear me say my prayers and make my face better by the morning.'

PARENTS' ATTITUDE TO THE SCHOOL

Parents were asked how long their child had been attending the special school and this information is presented below:

Period of attendance	No. of children
5–6 years	16
2–4 years	23
under 2 years	11

To obtain some indication of the parents' attitudes towards the school for physically handicapped children, the question was asked: 'Are the parents satisfied that, considering his defect, the child was reasonably excluded from ordinary school?' Forty-nine of the mothers answered 'yes', and one qualified this by saying 'but not at the time'. This was the mother of the boy with epispadias, who had previously been in an ordinary school where difficulties had arisen because of his incontinence. His teacher, unaware of his physical defect, had punished him (by shutting him in a cupboard) for being 'lazy and dirty .

To the following question: 'Did you appeal against his exclusion?' two mothers answered 'yes'. One was the mother mentioned above, who now expressed herself as satisfied; the other was the very difficult and psychologically disturbed mother of the haemophilic boy (Case 49), who said she had appealed 'frequently'. She added that she would have liked to have 'tried an ordinary school'. In her comments on the disadvantages of the special school, however, she remarked, 'He has to sit out and watch other children play,' which would, of course, have applied to a much greater degree in an ordinary school. This child was eventually transferred to a day open-air school because his mother could not bear his 'being with other children who are afflicted'.

Travelling Difficulties

Forty-eight parents stated that they had no travelling difficulties (Question 144). One complained about the length of time spent in travelling to and from the school, and one mentioned her child's travel sickness.

Travelling time naturally varied. Those who lived farthest away had to spend up to two hours travelling in the school bus each day, a considerable strain for any child and especially for those in calipers or otherwise disabled.

Disadvantages and Advantages

We also asked: 'What are the main disadvantages of the PH school?' Thirty-four parents replied that there were none; the remainder cited the following disadvantages. Seven mentioned 'not such good education', 'too wide an age range in classes', and similar themes. Three parents expressed the same idea in the form of a question, asking whether the education was as good as in ordinary schools. One parent commented on the schools' inability to recruit sufficient staff for still smaller classes—a valid criticism of an ideal school for handicapped children, but certainly not a fair comparison with an ordinary school. Three thought the children 'could be pushed a little more'. Two of these were mothers of children with dual defects, who found it difficult to accept the mental handicap in addition to the physical disability.

Of the two remaining 'disadvantages', one was expressed by a better-off mother who complained of 'the mixture of children and swearing'. Her criticism was directed, not unjustifiably, towards the child with the

severe haemangioma, fits and tantrums, who later improved. The final
'disadvantage' was: 'She wanted to go with her brother and sister to an
ordinary school, but has settled down now.'

The parents' responses to the question 'What are the main advantages
of the PH school?' can be broadly grouped as follows:

Advantages referred to	*No. of parents*
Good care and supervision	19
School transport	12
'The children are all the same, and not made to feel out of it.'	9
Smaller classes	5
Having a Sister on the premises	5
Medical care and availability of treatment	4
'They understand the children.'	4
'The children are happy in school.'	3
'The children are able to make friends and help each other.'	2
'The children accept the handicap more easily.'	2
'They make allowances for the handicap (sometimes too much).'	1
'They do everything possible.'	1
'They are very good to the children.'	1
'They teach them to be independent.'	1

CHAPTER 5

Social Problems

FAMILIES with a handicapped child face a number of special problems in their day-to-day living. This is inevitable; but what seems particularly unfortunate for the lower income groups is that the social problems they share with many other working class families, such as poor housing conditions, over-crowding and financial difficulties, bear more heavily on them *because* they have a handicapped child. This is a sphere in which a good deal could be done to lift the burden.

Hospital visiting over a long period, for instance, can prove a costly item in the family budget when it includes fares, the inevitable small presents for the child, and perhaps payment for the care of other children who have to be left at home. The cost and repair of special boots and shoes can also be heavy on the family purse (although the National Health Service covers the provision of surgical boots, it does not cover the provision and repair of special shoes which have to be adapted to the needs of the individual child).

Of all the social problems that must be faced, inadequate housing, in London at least, appears to be the most serious. For any mother with young children—and especially for a mother with a handicapped child—a small garden or even a yard, where the children can play in safety while she is busy, can make all the difference. Unless the family is lucky enough to live near a park, the only alternatives for play are the street, or the kitchen, which is often small and overcrowded, with the ever-present risk of burns and scalds. For this reason a flat or two or three rooms in a basement with a small garden or yard attached are much sought after, but this kind of accommodation, too, may have its disadvantages. Even where open space is accessible, it is not always made available. In one such case repeated letters to the local borough council resulted, not in permission to use the grass space available, but in two offers of much inferior accommodation with a small garden which were, not unnaturally, refused by the parents.

In another case, a family with two boys suffering from progressive muscular dystrophy (paralysis) lived in such a basement flat. Eight deep stone steps led down to it and there was a narrow spiral staircase up to the bedroom. The landlord, who lived in the flat above, objected to anyone using the tiny square of yard, so there was only the street or a nearby car dump. If the boys played in the street, they were taunted for being too lazy to run and play with the other children. How can a mother explain to every new child who arrives on the scene that although her children look normal, and even appear to have particularly well-developed calf muscles, they are partly paralysed? She would also have to explain that she takes them to the park in a pram or a push-chair not because they are babyish or lazy, but because they tire so quickly.

To add to these problems, the two rooms flooded in heavy rains and on three occasions had been flooded with sewage water from a man-hole in the passage; there was, of course, no compensation for carpets and furniture irreparably damaged. Small wonder that the older child, with these and other family problems in addition to his own, had severe temper tantrums and failed to make much progress at the child guidance clinic.

Numerous other examples could be given—the dangers to haemophilic children of playing in the street or the difficulties of carrying children with calipers up and down flights of stone stairs.

Problems of holidays and leisure facilities involve the whole family. Where can they take the handicapped child for a holiday—provided, of course, that they can afford one? 'It should be somewhere on the level, not too far from the sea, with not too many people to stare at him and a landlady who won't mind wet beds.' Imagine trying to find such accommodation in the school holiday period—and the price of it. Alternatively, imagine trying to keep a handicapped child happy and occupied, without a garden, for six or seven weeks in the summer, especially if he is an only child, or a difficult child, or in overcrowded conditions, or if it is necessary for the mother to have a job to help out with the family income.

There are play centres to help the mothers of ordinary children in the holidays, but it would be unrealistic to expect the play centre staff to accept the added responsibility of supervising handicapped children. It is easy to see what a boon a play centre for handicapped children would be, even if only for two or three times a week, provided there was the necessary transport such as there is in school time.

These are some, but by no means all, of the social problems every family with a handicapped child may face. We shall now look at some of them in greater detail as they were recorded in this survey.

The social class rating used by Tizard and Grad (1961) was adopted with the families classified as follows:

Non-manual	1
Skilled	18
Semi-skilled	12
Unskilled	19
Total	50

Of the fifty children in the survey only two came from so-called 'middle class' backgrounds. It is clear that the higher income groups are able to make other arrangements for their handicapped children.

Some of the families studied had severe financial difficulties. In two, the fathers had been unemployed for over a year through ill health. Both were receiving National Health insurance benefits supplemented by National Assistance. The widowed mother of one child worked as an assistant in the school but had to apply for National Assistance during the unpaid school holidays.

In four families the parents were divorced; in three of these the mothers were bringing up the children, and in the fourth, the father did so. In two cases the grandparents were bringing up the handicapped child.

A question on family income was included in the interview but as frequently several members of a family were working, and different methods were used to compute the housekeeping money, the answers became so complicated that any attempt to make accurate estimates would have taken a disproportionate share of the time for the whole interview. Nevertheless, it was found that twelve families, or nearly a quarter of those interviewed, apparently had a joint income of less than £10 a week.

Visiting and attending hospital

For low-income families, visiting a child in hospital over a long period and taking the eagerly-awaited presents of sweets, fruit, books or comics can be a substantial drain on resources. One mother stated that all the family savings had gone on visiting their only child in a county hospital miles away from home.

Handicap

Not all the difficulties associated with visiting a child in hospital, or attending hospital for supervision or treatment, were financial. In all, 64 per cent of the mothers experienced difficulties in this sphere, and the main reasons are listed below.

	No.
Time involved	25
Travelling	16
Cost of fares	13
Care of siblings	20
Parental ill health	8

In many cases the mothers mentioned more than one difficulty, as the following example shows.

Edwin was in a hospital specializing in the treatment of poliomyelitis, some miles out of London, for twelve and a half months. His mother quoted her expenses for weekly visiting:

Return fare (one parent)	10s.
Care of sibling all day (9.30 a.m.–4.30 p.m.)	10s.
Fruit, sweets (for child)	approx. 5s.
Bus fare to and from station each end	approx. 5s.

Thirty shillings a week for over a year can be a heavy burden in a household where there is not much margin for such extras, and Edwin's sister became resentful and jealous of the extra attention he was receiving while she was 'minded' in circumstances she disliked.

Five of the other children in the survey who had poliomyelitis had been admitted to this same hospital and several others went to long-stay hospitals even farther out of London. One of these was Charlie, who had a tuberculous spine and who remained in a hospital in the country for three years and ten months until his family could be rehoused in conditions which would not be detrimental to his health. Either his mother or his father managed to visit him almost every week throughout nearly four years, in spite of the fact that his father was an unskilled labourer and frequently unemployed. These visits, so vital to the child, must have entailed sacrifices from every other member of the family.

Renewal and Repair of Special Boots

Among other expenses incurred by the families of many handicapped children are those for the repair and renewal of special boots. Normal

TABLE 9 *Cost, Renewal and Repair of Special Boots*

Case No.	Condition	Boots renewed by	Frequency	Cost	Boots repaired by	Frequency	Cost	Delay	Difficulties	Comments
3	Talipes (bilateral)	Hospital	6 mo.	—	Grandfather (personally)	—	—	2–3 wks if hospital	Needs 2 prs for repairs	
5	Spastic	Hospital	6 mo.	—	Mother (Shop)	Every few wks	.	8 wks if hospital	Delay if hospital repairs	Has 2 prs
15	Poliomyelitis	Hospital	Every few mo.	—	Hospital	3 wks	1s. 10d. postage	3 wks repair	Financial (income under £10 per wk)	Needs 2 prs
18	Spastic	Mother (hospital adapts)	As necessary	—	Mother (Shop)	4 mo.	—	—	None	Mother gets new pair in advance
20	Osteomyelitis	Mother (hospital adapts)	4 mo.	£2 10s.	Mother (Shop)	3 wks	15s.	3–6 wks to adapt	Delay	Has 2 prs
36	Poliomyelitis	Mother (hospital adapts)	3 wks	£1 5s.	—	—	—	—	Financial (new shoes every 3 wks)	Found cheapest way
37	Talipes (bilateral)	Hospital	3–6 mo.	—	Mother (Shop)	2 wks	15s.	2–3 wks if hospital	Financial (under £10 per wk)	Too long if hospital repairs 2nd pair ruined
38	Spastic	Mother (hospital adapts)	9 mo.	£2 10s.	Mother (Shop)	2–3 wks	8s.	—	Financial (under £10 per wk)	Hospital boot unsatisfactory
40	Poliomyelitis	Mother (hospital adapts)	6 mo.	£3 7s.	Mother (Shop)	4 wks	13s.	—	Financial	Hospital boot unsatisfactory
43	Poliomyelitis	Mother (hospital adapts)	6 mo.	£2 4s.	Hospital	3 mo.	—	—	Financial	Odd sizes
50	Poliomyelitis	Mother (hospital adapts)	2 mo.	£2 3s. (1s. 10d. postage)	Hospital	2 wks	1s. 10d. postage	—	Financial (post every other week)	Has 3 prs

children, especially boys, have a reputation for going through their boots and shoes quickly. Many handicapped children appear to wear them out even more rapidly. This is often due to uneven weight-bearing in shoes which have been raised to correct a deformity but which very soon be-· come distorted and unwearable. The cost of renewal, adjustment and repairs is consequently extremely heavy.

Fourteen of the children in the survey required special boots. In eleven of these cases (see Table 9) the parents referred to difficulties in getting the boots renewed or repaired and seven explicitly mentioned the financial aspect; three of these families were in the under £10 a week income group.

Table 9 shows that in four cases the hospital provided the boots, and in seven the mothers themselves, with the hospital making the necessary adjustments. In two cases the mothers considered the hospital boots unsatisfactory: 'the toes came out in a week', etc.; and three mothers complained of long delays in repairs and adjustment. Two pairs were always necessary for this reason and one very lively and agile boy, who had poliomyelitis and was on crutches, had to have three pairs at a time, one pair being sent off every other week for repair.

HOUSING

Since the school was in London, housing accommodation, as might be expected, was an outstanding problem.

To the question 'Is there any way in which the authorities could make things easier for the parents of handicapped children?', twenty-nine mothers (58 per cent) answered in terms of a ground-floor flat with a garden. Only fifteen families had already found this type of accommodation. The remaining six families were less concerned with housing, but these were all cases in which the child's handicap was slight or temporary. Thus the majority of the parents considered a ground-floor flat and garden to be the top priority for a handicapped child and his family.

The reasons are obvious. The mother of a child with severe haemophilia remarked at the interview: 'If only Stephen had had a garden to play in, instead of the street, he wouldn't have had to go to hospital so many times.' This child had been in hospital more than thirty times. It would be interesting to estimate the cost to the Exchequer of his hospital admissions during the ten years that elapsed between the condemnation of the property in which the family lived and the provision of alternative accommodation—all this apart from the emotional effects on an already anxious mother and child. The family was eventually rehoused in a small house with a garden. The school staff noted a marked improvement in the child's health and social attitudes due in part, no doubt, to the relief of his mother's previously unremitting anxiety.

Many other examples could be given. In one case a severely spastic child had to be carried up and down to the fourth floor of a big block of flats without a lift, and there were the two young brothers with muscular dystrophy already referred to. Both these families have been re-housed to their satisfaction since the termination of the survey.

Table 10 presents some information about the living accommodation of the fifty families. The 'garden' mentioned was frequently only a small

TABLE 10
Housing Facilities

Facilities	None	Shared	Own
Bathroom	17	3	30
Inside WC	12	5	33
Kitchen/scullery	2	3	45
Bedroom	–	38	12
Garden	24	8	18

yard, although that, of course, was better than nothing. The problems of getting a severely handicapped child out for any length of time every day in a pram or a wheelchair, especially in the long holidays, are quite considerable, especially for mothers of large families or those who have to go out to work.

Seventeen of the families (34 per cent) had no bathroom. In one case the mother of three children, whose husband had deserted the family, had no hot water system. This meant that she had to heat every drop of water on the stove to wash or bath three children every night. The toilet, which was in the back yard, was shared with several other families.

Seven of these families have been rehoused satisfactorily since the investigation and have been most appreciative. The need for special care in rehousing families with a handicapped child, however, is illustrated by

Case 11. At the time of the pilot survey in 1959 George, a child with severe haemophilia and one leg paralysed from poliomyelitis, lived in two small furnished rooms in a basement with his parents and two younger brothers (one of whom also had haemophilia). When the family was re-visited for the survey in 1960 they had been moved to a pleasant little house and garden on a large new housing estate outside London. There was, however, no day school for physically handicapped children in the county and the family, quite understandably, resisted all attempts to send the two haemophilic children, then aged four and a half and seven, to a residential school. Home tuition for one hour four times a week was there-fore all that George could be given.

While the family was actually in the process of moving, Neil, the four-year-old brother with haemophilia, was in a London hospital with a bleeding episode. Within three days of moving George had a fall and had to be admitted to the children's hospital nearest to their new house. This was about seven miles away—a cross-country journey involving three different buses and taking about one and a half hours each way. It was difficult enough to visit him with a toddler and a new baby, but quite impossible to visit the younger child in London as well.

Later on, the two older children were constantly in and out of hospital with bleeding episodes. The third boy was normal, but the fourth also had haemophilia and the newest baby was awaiting assessment. The mother had been referred to a Catholic Marriage Guidance Clinic, which was unable to help her since irregular menstruation made the 'safe period' unreliable.

The housing estate itself was so large that the mother had to wait for a bus, which ran hourly, to take her to the main road, where she could get another bus to the hospital, the local maternity and child welfare clinic, or to the nearest orthopaedic clinic when the child with poliomyelitis had to be fitted for a caliper or receive supervision.

As a result of all these changes and difficulties George, who had been a lively happy child taking part in normal activities at school though in a walking caliper, at the second interview a year later appeared to be anxious, depressed and withdrawn—and had not walked since two days after leaving London. The initial fall in his new home had resulted in bleeding into the knee joint and he had been given a plaster shell which made walking impossible with the other leg in a caliper. By the time the plaster shell was removed the caliper was too small, and there followed a series of missed appointments owing to the circumstances described above and the mother's ill health during a new pregnancy. Minor mistakes at the clinic (where the difficulties of fitting a haemophilic child with a walking caliper were not at first appreciated) combined with many other factors, including a lack of physiotherapy and regular supervision, contributed to an overall deterioration in the situation.

The lack of a day school for physically handicapped children, the loss of all school interests and friends, anxiety about his inability to walk, and his virtual confinement to the house and small garden resulted in George's becoming 'a difficult child' and this naturally increased his mother's anxieties. At the second interview she appeared a worried and prematurely aged young woman. Her husband, who liked his new work and environment, remarked at the end of the interview that she frequently cried herself to sleep at night and that their relationship, which had previously been of the happiest, was becoming increasingly strained. Great efforts were made to get the family rehoused in London where the mother would have the much-needed support of her relations and friends and easy access to hospital and special day school. Unfortunately, this proved impossible owing to the shortage of accommodation. The local welfare authorities for the new housing estate worked unceasingly to try to overcome the numerous problems and the family, since the termination of the survey, has moved to a bungalow. This is near a local Roman Catholic day school which has accepted the two haemophilic boys for a trial period. The family like this new arrangement and appear a little more settled up to date, although the recurring crises naturally continue.

Thus the findings suggest that one outstanding need of families with handicapped children is for suitable housing accommodation. Yet the great majority of the children in the sample lived in poor, overcrowded accommodation or high up in large blocks of flats. It was usually impossible for the mothers to let the children play in the fresh air while they were busy with housework or a new baby, and outings required a special expedition.

LEISURE FACILITIES

A handicapped child may greatly restrict the holiday and leisure activities the family can undertake. The mothers often feel they cannot leave such a child in the care of ordinary baby-sitters.

Parents were asked whether their leisure activities were restricted in any way—that is, if they were any different from what they would be if the child were normal. Twenty-eight of the parents stated that their activities were 'not restricted', as against twelve who said they were 'severely restricted' and nine who included the handicapped child in their activities but found him 'a tie'. Thus over a third of the parents (42 per cent) reported that their leisure activities were severely restricted or that they found the child 'a tie'.

The responses to the following question suggest, however, that this proportion might be an underestimate and that some of the mothers may have been unwilling to admit how much the handicapped child restricted all their activities. This question was: 'How often does mother go out, for pleasure, without the child (e.g. friends, cinema, club, church)?' Almost half the mothers (46 per cent) answered that they never went out for pleasure without the child and another 24 per cent went out less than once a month (70 per cent in all).

In comparison, just over a quarter (28 per cent) of the fathers did not go out for pleasure without the child, but over a half (54 per cent) went out at least once a week.

It was interesting to note that eighteen of the mothers who 'never' went out were not among those who said that their leisure was restricted; they maintained that they would not have gone out in any case. On the other hand, nine mothers suggested spontaneously that if they could get a trained 'sitter-in' for their handicapped child (e.g. for a child who required help with toilet, or who had fits) it would enable them to go out occasionally with their husbands.

Holidays

Holidays are a break from routine which are obviously particularly important for families under the stress of caring for a handicapped child.

Item 48 asked whether the family's holiday arrangements were complicated in any way by the child, or whether the family had 'no holidays anyhow'. The responses were as follows:

	No.
Holidays complicated by the child	25
Have no holidays anyhow	18
It makes accommodation difficult to find	6
Financial difficulties	17

It was not easy to get a clear picture, but many mothers referred to the difficulty of finding suitable holiday accommodation because of the severity of the handicap and thus the child's sensitivity towards strangers, or because of enuresis, incontinence, or the need for a wheelchair. The majority appeared to have found a caravan holiday the best solution. It was evident that the families, and especially the fathers, had to accept many limitations and restrictions on their holidays. In 1961, however, the Council's scheme for 'recuperative holidays', arranged through the school, enabled fourteen children to have a seaside holiday who would otherwise have had to stay at home.

HOME VISITS BY SOCIAL WORKERS

The importance of home-visiting by trained social workers in relation to a school for physically handicapped children has already been discussed (p. 29). The multitude and variety of problems that face a family with a handicapped child demand that in addition to individual casework with the parents where this is required, continuous support should be available to the family from appropriate social work agencies.

A series of items was included about home-visiting and the parents' attitudes and reactions to home visitors. As with the questions relating to the number and frequency of hospital admissions, the parents had only hazy recollections of the number of times they had been visited and of the purposes of the visits. Accordingly, their responses were noted but analysis was restricted to their answers to only one question, which asked from what organizations their visitors came. The visitors were identified as follows:

	Responses
Invalid Children's Aid Association	42
School Care Committee	3
Children's Department	1
Family Welfare Office	1
Health Department (Health Visitor)	1
Family Service Unit	1
R.C. Church (lay worker)	1
Shaftesbury Society	1

These were the organizations remembered by the parents, but the records showed that many had in fact been visited from time to time by workers from other organizations as well, for different reasons; e.g. about holidays by the Shaftesbury Society, about free school dinners by the School Care Committee, and so on.

The analysis showed that caseworkers from the Invalid Children's Aid Association were visiting forty-two of the fifty cases in the survey. During the course of the interviews six cases were found to have had no regular home-visiting and the parents said that they would welcome it. They were therefore referred through the School Care Committee to the Invalid Children's Aid Association. The two remaining cases were, in fact, known to the Association and were visited occasionally by its workers as well as by the church worker and the family welfare worker referred to by the parents.

During the survey, therefore, all fifty cases were under the supervision of full-time, fully trained caseworkers from the Invalid Children's Aid Association. Visits were carried out weekly or fortnightly in cases with serious problems and at much longer intervals in other cases, according to need and at the request of the parents or school (see Chapter 10).

The majority of the cases (62 per cent) had been referred to the Invalid Children's Aid Association through the School Care Committee. Other sources of referral are given below:

Source of referral	No. of cases
School Care Committee	31
Hospitals	4
Divisional Medical Officer	3
School Medical Officer (from pre-school examination)	3
Health visitors	2
National Society for the Prevention of Cruelty to Children	1
National Spastic Society	1
A private physiotherapy clinic	1
Citizens' Advice Bureau	1
Family Welfare Association	1
Headmistress of the school	1

Social Problems

In an assessment of the value of home-visiting, the attitude of the parents to the visitors is a major factor. Item 149 asked, therefore, for the parents' views: thirty-four welcomed the visits, eight 'didn't mind', and only two resented them (the remaining six cases had not at the time been visited). Of the two who expressed resentment, one mother explained that the visits had coincided with her return from work, when she was busy getting the tea; she found them 'awkward'. The other mother, whose child had severe haemophilia, was one of the most difficult and psychologically disturbed mothers among the fifty families and was persistently unable to accept help or advice from any source. Her comment was that she 'felt the visits were a waste of time', although to an open question she suggested 'more education in handling the child and his problems' was needed by mothers of handicapped children in general.

The help and advice given is varied and practical and deals with housing, repairs of appliances, hospital appointments, transport, provision of escorts, assistance with clothing and special boots, holidays and outings. The central objective in every case, however, is to help the child and his family in making the adjustments needed to meet their problems and to accept the handicap.

Two general questions sought to discover to whom the parents would turn for help and support. One (Question 153) asked: 'To whom would the mother turn if she were ill and could not look after the child?'

	Responses
Relations, friends, or neighbours	42
School doctor/nurse	0
General practitioner	1
Social worker (specify)	7
Other	0

Among the forty-two who answered 'relations, etc.', two also gave the general practitioner, one the school doctor/nurse, and three added the Invalid Children's Aid Association. The seven who would turn to social workers specified workers from the Invalid Children's Aid Association, and one mother named the National Spastics Society also in this context.

The second question was: 'If the mother had any worries now that were connected with the child (e.g. his effect on parents' health, relationship with siblings, difficult behaviour), with whom would she discuss them?'

	Responses
Relations, friends, or neighbours	9
School doctor/nurse	15
General practitioner	7
Social worker (specify)	14
Other	5

Of the fourteen who would turn to social workers, nine specified workers from the Invalid Children's Aid Association, two named hospital almoners, two named workers from child guidance clinics and one selected a physiotherapist. In the category 'other' were a Health Visitor, a teacher, a psychiatrist, a hospital almoner and a hospital.

Allowing for some bias towards the school doctor and Sister, possibly out of consideration for the interviewer, it is clear that a substantial proportion of the mothers had sufficient confidence in the Invalid Children's Aid Association to turn to it as their first choice in an emergency.

GROUP PARTICIPATION

The feelings of isolation often experienced by the parents of a handicapped child have to a large extent, at least in London, been broken down by various organizations and associations of parents of children with different types of handicap. There is still a minority of parents who tend to hide their handicapped child because of their own feelings of guilt and shame, or their inability to face the stares and whispers of people outside their own intimate circle. And there may still be rare cases, especially in country areas, in which a handicapped child is hidden in an attic and never taken out.

The parents of severely handicapped children are often greatly relieved when they find an organization for others similarly placed. They begin to feel that they are not alone in their grief and perplexity. They discover that other people have the same kind of problems (sometimes even worse than their own) and have learnt somehow or other to cope with them and to find at least some measure of happiness for themselves and the children.

Accordingly, the parents in the survey were asked if they belonged to a parents' organization and, if so, to which. The answers are given opposite:

	No. of Parents
National Spastics Society	11
Haemophilia Society	2
Infantile Paralysis Fellowship	4
Muscular Dystrophy Group	1
	—
	18

In the course of the interviews and discussions, several parents who were not already members of any of these organizations asked to be put in touch with them. Thus the parents of seven children with cerebral palsy wanted to be introduced to the National Spastics Society, the parents of two children with haemophilia to the Haemophilia Society, and the parents of the child with muscular dystrophy to the appropriate group. These requests were met.

Few of the parents appeared to participate in other group activities. Although in twenty-two cases it was stated (Question 113) that one or both parents were practising members of a religion or church, only twelve parents attended church services regularly (once a week) and three attended 'occasionally'.

Only in three of the fifty families did the parents belong to any clubs or societies, one to an anglers' club, one to a judo club, and one (both parents) to a Salvation Army youth club.

These rather low figures may relate to the difficulties of leaving a handicapped child with neighbours or ordinary 'sitters-in'. 'Of course, my husband and I can never get out together' was a fairly frequent remark. The suggestion made by the interviewer, after hearing several such comments, that there might be a scheme to provide trained 'sitters-in' for handicapped children, was generally welcomed. There should be no great difficulty in organizing a voluntary rota through the Red Cross, St John Ambulance Brigade, various societies and associations for handicapped children, retired teachers and nurses, and so on to offer the parents of severely handicapped children an opportunity to go out together, perhaps once a month. This is the kind of service that might appeal strongly to voluntary workers and could bring much-needed relaxation to the parents of handicapped children.

CHAPTER 6

Emotional Problems of the Handicapped Child

A CHILD with a physical handicap is a child 'at risk' from the emotional point of view. He is, because of his handicap, 'different' from ordinary children. Most parents and children are aware of the need to be like everyone else; a need which is especially strong in one's school years. To have a handicap may mean to be deformed and perhaps disfigured. At worst, it may mean to be a freak or an oddity, and at best 'to have something *wrong*'—the very expression, so commonly used, implies some guilt or blame.

In any case, the handicap itself will be an object of curiosity to most people, evoking either their pity or their aversion and making it difficult for them to be at ease with the child concerned. People who are unsure of themselves in such a situation will tend to be over-emphatic, embarrassing the child with too much concern or pretending too obviously to ignore his difficulties. Even when a handicapped child is still too young to feel this almost universal attitude himself, his mother will have felt it for him and he will be affected by her reactions. She, too, may find it difficult to achieve a balance between over-anxiety and over-protection and may display some degree of real or apparent rejection. The latter may arise in part from the parents' disappointment at their 'failure' to have created, like all their friends and relations, a 'perfect' child.

One of the mothers in the survey, for instance, had a normal pregnancy and delivery and believed she had a perfect baby. On the fourteenth day of her baby's life she was told: 'Your baby will be a midget. She won't grow and you can't do anything about it.' The shock was so overwhelming, she said at the interview, that she had considered rejecting the baby altogether and could hardly bear to look at her. It was over six weeks before she could overcome this feeling. Her husband had by then helped her to realize that the child was their responsibility and that they 'couldn't hand her over to anyone else'. It is obvious how difficult it would be to overcome such deep feelings completely and in fact they reappeared in many different guises in the later relationship of mother and child.

Many parents spoke of their shame and embarrassment when people thoughtlessly turned to stare or to make audible remarks about their handicapped child—so much so that in some cases they avoided taking the child out as far as possible. The mother of one child who had multiple congenital defects admitted that for years she hid herself and the child in her own home. It was only shortly before the child came to school, when the mother accidentally met a school friend who also had a handicapped child, that she felt able to discuss her feelings and to take the child out with her. It is not difficult to understand how some physically and mentally handicapped children have been kept hidden for years, sometimes in one room, because their parents felt unable to acknowledge their 'shame' and believed themselves to be unique in their misery.

Some feelings of guilt and shame appear to be almost universal in the parents of handicapped children, and these feelings may affect the child's emotional development. In one or two instances fathers who were present at the interview were eager to stress that they did not care what other people thought. They appeared to have developed an armour of aggression towards the outside world to protect themselves and their child. These reactions could be seen reflected or exaggerated in some of the children, making it more difficult for them to accept their handicap and to develop an easy relationship with other children.

As the child grows older he becomes aware for himself that he is different. He must then start the long process of adapting himself to his handicap. At first he naturally wants to know *why* he is different and if he will ever be 'better', i.e. like other children: 'Shall I be able to walk and run and play?', 'Shall I always have to be in a chair?', 'What shall I do when I'm grown up?'. If he is an elder child, and the new baby can crawl and toddle, and eventually walk, he will want to know why the baby can do all the things that he cannot do. So the long series of crises in emotional adjustment goes on. Through these the child either learns to accept his limitations or to resent them. He may become depressed and anxious in accepting them or aggressive and difficult because he cannot accept them and resents the everlasting frustrations they impose.

Sooner or later, the handicapped child will also become aware of his special position in the family. He may be a source of resentment to his brothers and sisters because he gets more attention than they do; because he is an embarrassment to them and their friends; or because his handicap prevents the family from going on holiday, or having the kind of holiday they would like. He may consciously or subconsciously use his disability to get his own way, or he may withdraw to try to escape the strains of his relationships with other people.

He may also perceive only too well the difficulties his handicap has caused his parents, difficulties which not infrequently lead to the break-up of the family. One or other parent, usually the mother, may become pre-occupied with the handicapped child to the exclusion of everything else, or there may be mutual resentment between the parents over differences in their attitudes towards his problems. Their difficulties may be exacerbated by the extra work and stresses involved in caring for such a child; by their lack of opportunity to relax together, or to lead the life of a normal family. The marvel is not that a few of these families break down under the strain, but rather that so many are able to make the necessary adjustments and to give their handicapped child a happy and stable background which, in turn, helps him to accept his limitations.

Perhaps the heaviest anxiety of all, for both parents and child, relates to the child's future. 'Shall I be able to go to work and have a family like other people?' And the unspoken fear: 'If not, what is going to happen to me?' Responses (Question 52) showed that the problem of what will happen to the child in the future if one or both parents die, arouses the deepest distress and fear. Several mothers answered that they *did not* think about it and added, a moment later, that they *dare not* think about it. These were the mothers who saw only the prospect of an institution for the children for whom they had sacrificed so much, because there was no one in the family who would accept responsibility for them. There was a great difference in the outlook of these mothers compared with those who were confident that relatives would care for their child.

Apart from this question of the ultimate care of the child, the more immediate problems of special training and of getting and *holding* a suitable job are formidable enough. One of the tragedies of the present situation is that considerable numbers of handicapped children who have been given specialized training in a sheltered environment, such as a special day or residential school, find themselves as school leavers unable to compete in the open market—unable to use their hard-won skills to earn their own living.

It is now more widely acknowledged that a severe congenital abnormality or physical handicap is, of itself, an emotional hazard. To accept the limitations set by a severe handicap on day-to-day living and on their hopes for the future both parents and children clearly need considerable emotional resources and powers of adjustment, and many will need expert guidance and support.

In short, the recognition of a congenital abnormality or an acquired physical handicap of any severity involves an emotional crisis, and further crisis situations will inevitably occur from time to time. How these crises are resolved will depend on many factors, some of which may be subject to outside influence. In the first place, however, their outcome depends on the strength and flexibility of the relationships within the family and the support its members can give each other.

In recent years this area has been the subject of increasing attention. Reference has been made to an investigation carried out in the United States (Caplan, 1961) in a hospital where a thousand new children a year attend for physical handicaps. It was found that 'all . . . have some form of emotional complications, and many . . . have explicit psychiatric symptomatology'. The findings of the present survey also revealed many emotional complications associated with the handicaps. Specifically, information was sought in the following areas:

(i) the prevalence and severity of emotional problems in the children themselves;

(ii) the prevalence and severity of emotional problems in their parents and siblings;

(iii) factors adversely affecting the emotional adjustment of handicapped children and their families;

(iv) the forms of treatment, supervision, and support given to the children and their families.

THE PREVALENCE OF EMOTIONAL PROBLEMS IN HANDICAPPED CHILDREN: REFERRALS FOR CHILD GUIDANCE

The actual referral rate for child guidance in the fifty cases studied was 24 per cent. This is three times the average rate of referral from ordinary schools as estimated from their pilot surveys undertaken by the Underwood Committee (Ministry of Education, 1955). This high rate is in itself an indication of the extent and severity of the emotional problems—provided that the referrals were not due to personal bias in those responsible for them, or to special interests engendered by the survey.

TABLE II
Referrals for Child Guidance: Age and Symptoms

Case No.	Referred by	To Whom	Through	Age	Main Symptoms	Date of Referral	Comments
2	SMO (mother's request)	CGC	Direct	12	Behaviour problems sexual precocity	1960	During survey interview
5	SMO	CGC	PCC	10	Anxiety, depression	1959	Following school conference
13	SMO and Educ. psychol.	CGC	PCC	10	Anxiety, depression	1960	Following school conference (6 mo. before survey)
20	DMO (mother's request)	Consult. Psychiat. (hospital)	Direct	7	Nocturnal enuresis	1959	Request for intra-hospital referral
21	SMO	Consult. Psychol. (hospital)	Direct	9	Anxiety, tension, inability to learn	1959	Following school conference
24	Consult. physician (hospital)	Consult. Psychiat. (hospital)	Direct	3	Severe temper tantrums, aggression	1958	Pre-school recommendation
31	SMO	Consult. Psychiat. (hospital)	PCC	10	Temper tantrums, aggression	1960	Prior to survey interview; guidance had been refused for 2 years
35	Consult. Physician (spastics centre)	CGC	Direct	6	Temper tantrums, aggression	1959	Pre-school recommendation
41	Consult. Physician (hospital)	Consult. Psychiat. (hospital)	Direct	5	Anxiety, enuresis and encropresis	1958	Requested following school conference
42	SMO	CGC	PCC	8	Anxiety, withdrawal	1959	Referred 6 mo. after transfer to PH school
47	Dr (maternity and child welfare clinic)	CGC	Direct	4	Temper tantrums, aggression	1959	Pre-school recommendation
49	Consult. Physician (hospital)	Educ. Psychol. (hospital)	Direct	5	Anxiety, withdrawal	1960	Prior to survey interview, child guidance had been refused for 3 years

SMO = School Medical Officer   DMO = Divisional Medical Officer
CGC = Child Guidance Clinic   PCC = Problem Cases Conference
PH = Physically Handicapped (school)

Table 11 gives details of how the children were referred and to whom, at what age and with what main symptoms. The dates of referral are given and brief comments included. These cases are all discussed in greater detail in Chapter 10.

The table shows that four children were referred by the school doctor, following full discussions at school medical examinations, to Problem Cases Conferences with a view to child guidance—the normal course of procedure. These four had all been referred before the survey interview took place.

Two children were referred directly for psychiatric treatment by the school doctor. One referral (Case 2) was arranged after the survey interview in the course of which the mother asked if the child could go to the child guidance clinic his brother had attended. The question had already been under consideration for about a year before the interview. The consultant surgeon under whose care the child remained (following a depressed fracture of the skull and right hemiplegia) had been approached for his agreement for child guidance. He had, however, first referred the child to a neurologist and the behaviour problems had worsened. In the second case (Case 21, the child with spastic paraplegia following TB meningitis) the direct referral to a hospital psychiatric department was made after lengthy discussions with the school staff and educational psychologist because the parents resisted the idea of a child guidance clinic.

Three children were referred by their own hospital consultants to the psychiatric departments of the hospitals concerned, another was referred by the divisional medical officer at the mother's request, another by the doctor at a maternity and child welfare clinic before the child reached school age, and one by the consultant physician at a spastics centre which the child attended before she came to school.

The nature of the problems presented by the children referred for child guidance showed that most of them were related directly to their handicaps and would therefore probably occur to a greater or lesser degree among many, if not all, of the children attending the school.

ASSESSMENT OF CHILDREN'S EMOTIONAL ADJUSTMENT

To assess the frequency of these and other signs of failure to make a satisfactory adjustment and to estimate their severity, scoring standards were designed for both parents and children. These were based on the groupings of symptoms considered in the Underwood Report to be indicative of some degree of maladjustment, and were discussed in detail with Professor Tizard of the Medical Research Council Social Psychiatry Research Unit.

Signs of difficulty in the children in adjusting to their handicaps were classified as follows:

(i) nervous disorders: inhibited, anxious or withdrawn reactions;

(ii) habit disorders, involving some disorder of speech, sleep, movement or excretion;

(iii) behaviour disorders: aggressive, troublesome or delinquent reactions.

For many of the symptoms listed any and every manifestation does not indicate failure to make a good adjustment, but only manifestations that are excessive, abnormal or unduly frequent.

Adjustment was evaluated from responses to selected items in the survey questionnaire revealing the child's reactions as seen by the parent to the problems created by his handicap, and from the responses to similar items selected from the teachers' questionnaire revealing his reactions as seen by the teacher (Appendix II).

For both sets of items the total number of scoring points over the three disorder groups—nervous, habit and behaviour—was twenty-four.

The methods of scoring, from both the survey and the teachers' questionnaire, are presented in Appendix III A, B, C.

Since these assessments were in some degree subjective and the borderline difficult to define, the responses were not weighted. An over-anxious mother will describe her child as 'extremely nervous', whereas one who wishes to minimize the difficulties or present a favourable picture may choose the more moderate 'rather nervous or timid'. In both instances it was felt that a departure from normal attitudes had been noted and both responses were therefore scored.

Scores were interpreted in the following way. Out of the total number of scoring points of 24 for the three disorder groups, nervous, habit and behaviour,

scores of 0–1 were considered to indicate *normal* reactions;

scores of 2–3 were considered to indicate *slight* emotional difficulties relative to the handicap;

scores of 4–5 were considered to indicate *moderately severe* emotional difficulties;

scores of 6 and over were considered to indicate *severe* emotional difficulties and failure to adjust.

The interpretations are necessarily arbitrary and personal and are best indicated by an anchoring illustration.

AN EXAMPLE OF SEVERE EMOTIONAL DIFFICULTIES *(Case 2)*

Case 2, Lionel, was the boy with a right hemiplegia and slight mental retardation following a fall of twenty feet through the glass roof of a garage on to a concrete floor when he was four and a half years old. He sustained a depressed fracture and was unconscious for twenty-one days. Part of the left parietal bone was removed but no plate was considered necessary. He remained in hospital for five months and was discharged with a right hemiplegia.

Table 12 presents his scores in the three disorder categories. It will be seen that he showed six signs of failure to adjust in the group of behaviour disorders from both questionnaires. These are listed in Appendix III A and B.

TABLE 12
Lionel: Adjustment Score

	Survey questionnaire		Teachers' questionnaire	
	Lionel's score	possible score	Lionel's score	possible score
Nervous disorders	0	5	1	7
Habit disorders	0	10	1	6
Behaviour disorders	6	9	6	11
Total	6	24	8	24

With a total score in the survey questionnaire of six out of twenty-four signs of failure to adjust, and in the teachers' questionnaire of eight out of twenty-four, this child was considered to have severe emotional difficulties.

DIFFERENCES BETWEEN PARENTS' AND TEACHERS' ASSESSMENTS
OF CHILDREN'S ADJUSTMENT

However carefully the indications of emotional difficulties are selected for assessment by the parent and the teacher, there are obvious reasons why the results should show considerable variance. In general, the observations of the teachers are likely to be more objective. Since the mother is emotionally involved she may, consciously or subconsciously, minimize her difficulties or even fail to recognize them, or alternatively she may exaggerate them through over-anxiety. On the other hand, a child who shows behaviour disturbance at home may respond quite differently to the control and discipline of school and so tend to obtain a lower score.

In fact, it is interesting to note that in thirty-three of the forty-eight cases[1] the teachers' responses resulted either in a higher score of emotional disorders than the mothers' (twenty-seven cases) or in the same score (five cases), and in only sixteen cases did the teacher's observations give a lower score.

The disparity between the scores, though relatively slight, appears to reflect the objectivity of the teacher's answers as against the more subjective and defensive answers of the mother. The mother's responses could be seen as an attempt, perhaps, to put a good face on it, or as unwillingness to admit to difficulties in handling the child at home. For these reasons the teachers' assessments were considered the more reliable and they, rather than the mothers' estimates, were used in the cases where the two scores differed.

Given the likelihood of obtaining differing assessments of the children's adjustment from two such different approaches as that of the parent and that of the teacher, and in two such different settings as the home and the school, the correlation coefficient of 0·29 shows a basis of agreement on the extent of the emotional difficulties the children were experiencing in relation to their handicaps. Some of the individual cases in which the parents' and the teachers' estimates differed are discussed in Appendix VI.

CONCLUSION

With this measure of agreement between the mothers' and teachers' independent assessments it is possible to make a rough estimate of the degree of maladjustment or, more exactly, of failure to make a satisfactory adjustment among the fifty children in the survey. From the scores obtained; five children (scores 0–1) came within the category of *normal* reactions; seventeen (scores 2–3) were experiencing *slight* emotional diffi-

[1] The teachers' questionnaire was not completed for two children. One had been included in the initial pilot study and had subsequently left, and the teacher did not remember him well enough to undertake the questionnaire. The other had been too short a time in school for the teacher to express an opinion.

culties relative to their handicap; thirteen (scores 4–5) showed *moderately severe* difficulties; and fifteen children (scores of 6 and over) showed *severe* difficulties and failure to adjust. Thus twenty-two (44 per cent) of the children showed normal or slight emotional difficulties in adjusting to their handicaps and twenty-eight (56 per cent) showed moderate to severe emotional difficulties in adjusting to their handicaps.

Some support for these findings is seen in the referrals for child guidance. Of the twelve children who were attending for child guidance, seven were in the group with severe emotional problems and three showed symptoms of moderate severity (one of these was successfully treated and is now under supervision). One child (Case 20) was in the category for slight emotional difficulties and was said by the psychiatrist to have 'remained emotionally healthy and undamaged to a surprising extent' despite five years of chronic osteomyelitis and at least twenty-six admissions to hospital (including five major operations) since he was three and a half years old. He was nevertheless attending a consultant psychiatrist for persistent enuresis. The remaining child (Case 5), though scored as normal, had been referred by the school doctor for child guidance because of his initial difficulties in settling at school and his persistent vomiting.

Further details of the children referred for child guidance are given in Chapter 10.

There appeared to be little correlation between the different types of disorder—nervous, habit and behaviour—in the mothers' and teachers' estimates, except in two cases of pronounced behaviour disorders. In general, the symptoms recorded appeared to come from each of the three groups singly or together, without differentiation.

CHAPTER 7

Emotional Problems of the Parents
and Siblings

As HAS been pointed out, a severe physical handicap or congenital abnormality in a child is a source of strain for all the members of the family, particularly, of course, for the parents. The crises that arise may be resolved by the family alone or with the help of outside agencies; they may remain unresolved or only partially resolved, and manifest themselves as emotional anxiety in the members of the family or in their failure to accept the handicap.

Caplan (1961) found that one of the most emotionally stressful periods for every mother is the first three to four weeks after leaving the lying-in hospital. During these weeks before she can visit the baby clinic she may be left to her own resources, unless she is lucky enough to have a supporting family around her. This period may consequently be productive of a good deal of insecurity, especially if the parents or grandparents come from different cultural backgrounds and 'everyone in the family, not to mention the neighbours, is telling the mother something different'.

If there is 'something wrong' with the baby, such as prematurity or a congenital abnormality, the anxiety and tension may be increased enormously. It is usually many months, and may even be years, before the parents see any specialized agency with experience in the problems of handicapped children, such as the Crippled Children's Services in the United States or the Invalid Children's Aid Association and similar organizations in this country. During this period the parents 'have to deal *unaided* with the complicated emotional burden of adapting to the child's abnormality'. Caplan continues: 'How much time and wasted professional energy would be saved, not to mention avoidable unhappiness and personality distortions for family and child, if community leaders were to realize that a baby with a congenital abnormality is a situation requiring emergency agency attention concentrated and deployed at the critical period; that is, within the first two months of birth.'

It is impossible to talk to the parents of a handicapped child for any length of time without becoming aware of the shock and agony of mind which many of them have passed through during those first critical weeks. They have had to face their families and in-laws, their neighbours and, most painful of all perhaps, themselves, with a baby who is not quite perfect and may even be deformed.

Mention has already been made (p. 76) of some of the initial difficulties of the mother whose child was born 'a midget'. Even after the first shock these parents had to go on making efforts to adjust themselves to the situation without specialized help or guidance until the child came to school. When the mother and child were first seen at school it was clear they had many emotional problems and the mother welcomed the offer of help from a trained caseworker. In fact, however, she proved unable to bring herself to discuss her problems and always managed to be out or not to hear the bell when visited at home. On the one or two occasions when she saw the caseworker she could only talk about the problems of an over-indulgent grandmother and was quite unable to discuss her own feelings about the child.

For the parents of a child with multiple handicaps the shock is proportionately greater and the period of diagnosis may be agonizingly prolonged, as in Mary's case (Case 19). The mother already had one child, a boy with a hare lip born three years before Mary. During her second pregnancy she had suffered from severe depression and backache following the death of her father and the breakdown of her mother. The baby was delivered by a midwife at home, after a long labour, and weighed only four pounds. Her own doctor was called in the day after the confinement and told her of the baby's cleft palate. He also advised her to take the baby to hospital for advice about a swelling over her spine. On the fourteenth day after the confinement the mother herself took the baby to the local children's hospital. She learned that Mary had a spina bifida and would probably be paralysed from the waist down. When the baby was five months old the mother was told at the welfare clinic that there was also some abnormality of the heart and the child was again referred to hospital.

In relating all this at the interview the mother said that she felt she would never come to the end of being told of new disabilities and that she would have preferred to have known them all from the beginning. Even at eleven months, when the child was examined in hospital for her heart condition, the sum of her disabilities was not yet complete. She was found to have congenital dislocation of one hip, severely deformed feet, epilepsy and some degree of mental impairment. Finally, when she reached school it was discovered that she also had a hearing defect. Had this mother known the full extent of the child's disabilities from the beginning, the knowledge might well have been unendurable. Small wonder that for years she hid herself and her child in her own home, so that few of her relations or friends were aware that she had a handicapped child.

For all this, few mothers could have given their children greater care and attention. When Mary was strong enough to stand the first stage of the operation for repair of the palate, she was admitted to a hospital a good way outside London and her parents visited her daily, from July to mid-December, on a motor-bike with sidecar. The mother described the strain on her husband, after the day's work, of driving out to the hospital in all weathers, and of how on weekdays they were allowed only to peep at the child, unseen, because she was so upset when they left. Only at the weekends were they allowed to sit with her, because then the visiting time was longer.

She talked of her own difficulties in coping with the handicap: of such practical tasks as washing twelve to fourteen nappies every day for thirteen years; of her feelings; and of how painful she found it when other people, especially children, stared at Mary. Her older son was also affected by the situation. He became shy and withdrawn and never brought his friends home. The family was severely restricted with regard to leisure activities and holidays, and because of Mary's incontinence only caravan holidays were feasible. For all these reasons, and because of the overwhelming fear of another pregnancy, marital relations reached breaking point.

Asked what she found most distressing about having a handicapped child, her mother replied: 'Heart-breaking altogether. She has been done out of so much.' Yet she managed to say of the child: 'She is a real trier. She copes very well and is very cheerful.' It is not difficult to imagine the severity and frequency of the emotional crises this family have had to face, nor how great their need for skilled and sympathetic support. Yet it was not until Mary was six and a half years old, and strong enough to come to school, that they were referred for such support. Thereafter the child was visited weekly or fortnightly in her own home and her mother was able to discuss the difficulties with a trained and sympathetic case-worker. Clearly, support of this kind would have been even more valuable during the first few weeks and months, as the parents became aware of the problems they would have to face. She herself made this point when she said to the visiting caseworker: 'If only we'd known you a few years ago, when we most needed your help.'

This theme, in almost the same words, was repeated again and again by the mothers of children referred for specialized help from trained caseworkers when they reached school age. But it should be clear to all concerned that such help is most needed, and can be of the greatest value, *immediately a handicap is recognized.*

When a child is born with a handicap in hospital, or when a child is found with a handicap, congenital or acquired, the hospital authorities should inform the public health service as well as the general practitioner so that arrangements can be made for help and advice in the home. The Health Visitor, in the normal course of home-visiting, should be a second line of defence for handicapped children under five. She should ensure that the local authority is immediately made aware of every handicapped child in its area. The child should then be included on an 'at risk' register for periodic review by the medical officer in charge and for consideration of all the special needs of the family, including the need for specialized casework.

Although in every case the problems differed, the handicap itself clearly involved an emotional crisis for the parents. Where they had been told that the prognosis was grave, or that the child would be unlikely to survive adolescence, the strains and tensions appeared almost unbearable.

In the case of inherited diseases, such as haemophilia, the parents' profound sense of guilt created its own emotional complications, and this was marked in three of the four cases of haemophilia included in the survey. (In the fourth, the child had been adopted by private agreement and the condition was not suspected or recognized until he was nearly a year old.)

In Case 42, for example, it appeared that Terry's parents had married because he was expected. His mother was just seventeen and perhaps only vaguely aware of the implications of her own father's mild haemophilia. Terry's haemophilia, however, was severe, and the husband never failed to make his wife aware of her responsibility for the recurring crises in the life of their only child. Terry was admitted to hospital with uncontrolled bleeding thirty times before he was seven years old.

In the face of circumstances such as these, it was not surprising to find that in addition to the twelve children and their parents who had been referred for child guidance, six parents were receiving psychiatric therapy.

Handicap

Two mothers were attending hospital for psychiatric treatment and two saw a psychiatrist regularly; two fathers were suffering from acute anxiety states and attending hospital. In a seventh case, a father was suffering from chronic anxiety and a duodenal ulcer and was under regular treatment from his own doctor. There was much additional chronic physical and mental ill health among mothers and fathers, which obviously both reflected and increased their anxieties (see Chapter 9).

The problems presented by parents receiving therapy were also found among those who had no treatment. These problems appeared directly attributable to their common situation as parents of handicapped children. For this reason, therefore, a similar assessment was made of the emotional difficulties of the parents as for the children.

ASSESSMENT OF PARENTS' EMOTIONAL DIFFICULTIES

The parents' emotional difficulties were classified as *over-anxiety, depression* and *over-protection*, on the one hand, and *rejection, friction* and *aggression* on the other. Over-anxiety was estimated from the responses to eight items in the survey questionnaire relating to reactions and attitudes: rejection was estimated from the responses to four items in the survey questionnaire and four items in the teachers' questionnaire. (See Appendix IV.)

As with the children, every manifestation of a symptom does not indicate failure to make a good adjustment; only manifestations that are excessive, abnormal or unduly frequent are significant. As before, the responses are not weighted. Thus to Question 73: 'Is mother very depressed?', responses 2 ('frequently') and 3 ('always') each scored one point.

REJECTION

Four questions from the teachers' questionnaire were selected which might give some indication of rejection. These were:

Question 13 (a): Have you discussed this child's education with either of his/her parents during the past year?
Question 13 (b): To what extent do this child's parents show interest in his/her progress at school?

Answers of 'neither' in the first case and 'little or no interest' in the second each scored one point, indicating some rejection.

The other two more open questions were:

Question 9: Do you consider that this child's school work is adversely affected by any factors outside the school (e.g. home circumstances, out of school activities, etc.)?

Question 24: Please comment on any problems of adjustment or conduct which are, or might be, a cause of concern.

If the teacher commented adversely on the influence of home circumstances in her answer to either of these questions, each counted one point.

In estimating the extent of rejecting attitudes, therefore, it was possible to see whether there was a measure of agreement between the parents' and the teachers' responses to the four items selected from the survey questionnaire and the teachers' questionnaire respectively.

It is obvious that many factors would influence the answers to these two sets of questions on attitudes of rejection. For example, in Case 7, when the child did not live with her parents, the guardian (grandmother) rather naturally represented the situation as entirely satisfactory and said that the child remained with her from choice and was perfectly happy. The teacher, however, noted: 'Does not live with parents but with grandparents. Earlier on, this caused tension and subsequent reactions; this factor seems to have solved itself to some degree, and Rosemary is a much happier and better adjusted child than two years ago.' Nevertheless, the answers to the other three questions reflected some lack of interest and the teacher's score for rejection was four.

Nevertheless, taking the many possible variations into consideration the results were remarkably close in the forty-eight cases in which the two estimates were made.[1] The findings corresponded exactly in twenty-four cases and in a further fifteen the scores from the two questionnaires differed by only one point. Thus there was a considerable measure of agreement in just over 81 per cent of the cases, Appendix VII discusses the nine cases in which the discrepancies were greater than one point.

Scores for rejecting attitudes from the two sets of four questions were interpreted as follows. Out of four signs of rejection:

scores of o were considered to indicate *normal* reactions;
scores of 1 were considered to indicate *slight* rejection;
scores of 2 were considered to indicate *moderate* rejection;
scores of 3 or 4 were considered to indicate *severe* rejection.

Since the interpretations are necessarily arbitrary and personal, cases illustrating the different degrees of rejection are described here.

[1] Cf. p. 84 above.

Handicap

A Slight Degree of Rejection (Case 23)

This child had achondroplasia (Dwarfism). To Question 107: 'Does mother ever feel ashamed and embarrassed by people knowing about the child's handicap?', the mother's answer at the survey interview was 'Yes', and she added that she felt aggressive if people stared. This mother had openly admitted her initial rejection of the child when told of her handicap in hospital.

The teacher's comment, which scored one point on the measure of rejection, was that the child 'seems to be allowed to decide what she likes to eat, to the point of being indulged', possibly indicating an attempt by the mother to compensate for her rejection of the child.

A Moderate Degree of Rejection (Case 31)

This child had an atrial septal defect with pulmonary hypertension and scoliosis. The mother said that both she and the father felt ashamed and embarrassed at people knowing about the child's handicap because 'she is so small', which the mother seemed to interpret as a reflection on her care. In fact, this attitude was revealed in answers to many other questions during the interview. One of the comments made by the school doctor on writing up the interview shortly afterwards was: 'Mother disinclined to discuss the question, "How has the child affected the marriage relationship?" (Question 103), but the child's disability and the parents' lack of acceptance have undoubtedly produced considerable tension and difficulties.'

After prolonged casework the child's father was also invited to the school. He came on one occasion and the parents then agreed, with some reluctance, to the need for child guidance. At the diagnostic interview the psychiatrist reported of the mother: 'She did not like the idea at all. After all, what mother would?' He found the child 'very depressed and full of resentment and in need of psychotherapy . . . although the mother's hostility, at least during this interview, was not nearly so extreme as might have been expected from the reports, she was able to tell me how fed up her husband was with Katie and her incredibly obstinate behaviour'. This mother, however, proved unable to accept regular child guidance; she attended only two or three times but agreed that she would go back if the situation seemed to be deteriorating. It was clear from the beginning that both she and her husband would find it very difficult to tolerate any recognition of their own attitude of rejection; it was equally clear that the child was in great need of psychiatric help. The school case-worker continued home visits at the request of the psychiatrist.

The teacher's recognition of the situation was revealed in her answer to Question 9: 'Do you consider that this child's school work is adversely affected by any factors outside the school (e.g. home circumstances, out-of-school activities, etc.)?' The teacher's response was: 'Yes. Attitude of parents to Katie and her brother.' Katie's jealousy of her normal brother was recognized by everyone concerned with her at school, and Katie told the psychiatrist, 'Mother and father both liked him better than me.' Again, to Question 24, which asked the teacher to comment on any problems of adjustment or conduct which are or might be a cause of concern, the teacher answered: 'The whole situation is still fraught with difficulties. Katie's behaviour problems have become easier this year, but I feel that there is still an underlying tension. This may break again on removal to secondary school.' (The teacher's fears were subsequently realised.)

A Severe Degree of Rejection (Case 6)

In this case, a child with spastic paraplegia and dysarthria, the parents were separated and a divorce was pending. The mother declared that the effect of the child on the marriage relationship had been to make it worse: 'Father was ashamed of her and took no part in caring for her.' This was a particularly difficult case. The prevailing symptoms were constipation at eighteen months and delay in talking up to four years of age. The mother was Rhesus-negative and arrangements had been made for an exchange transfusion. The baby was, however, born before the mother's arrival in hospital and transfusion was not considered necessary. The mother was anxious about the child's development from eighteen months when she first took her to hospital, since there was a history of mental defect in her family. She was told that the child was 'just born lazy' and suffered from double incontinence. The family moved when she was four years old and attended another hospital, where a diagnosis of spastic diplegia and dysphagia was made. Physiotherapy and speech therapy were given and the incontinence was treated and somewhat improved.

When the child was seven years old the father deserted under particularly distressing circumstances, for his children saw him frequently with his new 'wife' and were ignored by him. The mother, whom we saw shortly after the break, was deeply unhappy and Rosalind, who was especially fond of her father, relapsed again into double incontinence and developed temper tantrums. Her sister contracted rheumatic fever.

The mother, after trying several unsuitable housekeeping jobs, finally became a caretaker for a block of flats and was able to make a real home for the children. She has made a good adjustment, and the child and her sister have improved steadily. The mother is aware of the possible need for child guidance at a later date, but is rather opposed to it at present 'unless it is absolutely necessary'.

The teacher's observations were that neither parent had discussed the child's education with her during the past year and that they showed little or no interest in her progress at school (possibly owing to the mother's difficulty in getting time off work to come to the school). The teacher also considered that the child's school work was adversely affected by 'disturbed home life'. She added: 'Bad maladjustment, which is beginning to be overcome. Much happier and more contented of late but still much tension.' Her final comment (to Question 24) was that the child 'needs affection and friendliness if the improvement in her adjustment is to continue. She is still immature and needs a lot of help to grow up.'

The 'rejection' in this case clearly refers to the father only. The child has since moved to a secondary school and the home is still visited by the caseworker.

Summary

From the scores obtained:

seventeen parents showed *no rejection* of their children (scores of o);
eighteen showed some *slight* rejection (scores of 1);
eight showed a *moderate* degree of rejection (scores of 2);
and seven showed a *severe* degree of rejection (scores of 3 or 4).

In twenty of the twenty-four cases in which different scores were obtained, the teachers' estimates of rejection, presumably more objective, were higher (see Appendix VI) and were therefore used.

The results indicate that in 31 per cent of the cases the parents showed moderate or severe degrees of rejection of their handicapped children.

Some independent confirmation of these estimates appears in the actual case histories. In three of the cases in the survey the father had left the family shortly after the birth of the handicapped child; in a fourth case the mother had deserted when her daughter returned from hospital with paralysis of one leg following poliomyelitis. In another case, first the father and then the mother had deserted the handicapped child after the grandfather had approached the National Society for the Prevention of Cruelty to Children because of the father's neglect and ill-treatment of the baby. In a sixth case the handicapped child was illegitimate and was brought up by the grandparents. In three other cases the father had left the family temporarily, but subsequently returned.

Actual rejection, therefore, temporary or permanent, occurred in 18 per cent. While the presence of the handicapped child may have been only an additional factor in an unsatisfactory marital relationship, it appeared to be a precipitating factor in all but one of these cases. Without comparable figures from ordinary schools it is impossible to draw any conclusion, but the percentage of broken families certainly appears high.

OVER-ANXIETY AND OVER-PROTECTION

Reactions in this category could be assessed only from responses to the survey questionnaire. Eight questions were selected for this purpose (see Appendix IV).

Question 71 asked: 'Is mother concerned about the health or behaviour of any other member of the family or household (state relationship to child)?' Only responses referring specifically to the father (anxiety, depression) have been scored in this context. Five questions (73, 74, 75, 76, 78) were concerned with the mother's reactions (depression, anxiety, insomnia, tension, fatigue). Finally, two questions asked directly about the parents' attitude to the child's disability. The first (Question 117) related to the mother: 'Is the mother able to cope with the handicap, having difficulty in coping with the handicap, or unable to cope with the handicap unaided?' (Either of the last two responses scored one point.)

Prompting questions on this item were:

> Does she try to ignore his disability?
> Does she urge him to overcome it?
> Does she protect him from difficulties?
> Does she encourage his independence?

Question 118 asked the same questions about the father.

Scores on the responses to these eight questions were interpreted as follows. Out of eight signs of over-anxiety, depression, and over-protection:

scores of 0–1 were considered to indicate *normal* reactions;

scores of 2 were considered to indicate *slight* over-anxiety relative to the handicap;

scores of 3–4 were considered to indicate a *moderately severe* degree of over-anxiety;

scores of 5 and over were considered to indicate a *severe* degree of over-anxiety.

Again, illustrations of these interpretations are offered below.

Normal Reactions (Case 28)

This child, the third in the family, after an apparently normal birth developed double pneumonia within twenty-four hours and was on oxygen continuously for ten days. She was discharged from hospital at sixteen days, but continued to attend until she was two. She was late in sitting and was making no attempt to stand at two years, and mother was told she was a 'lazy baby'. The mother then approached the local welfare clinic with a request for a letter to a children's hospital. Here she was diagnosed as 'spastic' and attended physiotherapy. She was admitted to the physically handicapped school at three years three months. At three years nine months she had a fall in the playground and was admitted to hospital with otitis media for a week. About a year later, mother noticed that her head was getting larger. She was re-admitted and had two operations for the insertion of a Spitz-Holtzer catheter and was kept in hospital for about five months.

She remained under the neurosurgical unit, and has 'turns' of severe headache and vomiting, lasting about six hours. The turns may occur from twice a week to every two months.

In spite of this history the parents showed a remarkable degree of adjustment and acceptance of the handicap, and their reactions were scored as normal, although mother was under treatment from her own doctor for a duodenal ulcer 'probably due to anxiety'. Her own comments threw light on some of the factors which had made this adjustment possible: 'Father has taken at least half of the job of bringing her up—puts her to bed every night', and in relation to the child, she 'makes the most of what she's got. Does things for herself, very independent'. The whole family appeared well adjusted, though they were anxious about Tessa's future and whether she would be able to work, and the parents felt their leisure activities were severely restricted because they could *never* go out together.

A Slight Reaction of Over-Anxiety (Case 20)

This mother complained of tension and anxiety, with very good reason. The child had chronic osteomyelitis and had been admitted to hospital twenty-six times since the age of three years eight months and had undergone five major operations. He had persistent enuresis, for which he attended a hospital psychiatric department. His elder brother attended the same hospital, also for anxiety and enuresis. The father had had a severe depression in 1955, the year after the boy's initial illness, but was given electro-convulsive therapy and made a good recovery.

The psychiatrist's report (quoted above) was that the boy 'has remained emotionally healthy and undamaged to a surprising extent . . . but has a tendency to babyishness and a dependent and passive attitude in relation to adults'. Of the mother, the psychiatrist said: 'shows her anxiety openly . . . and she has something to worry about.'

A Moderately Severe Degree of Over-Anxiety (Case 1)

This child had a congenital urethral stricture and bilateral hydronephrosis. The mother was an anxious woman and showed frequent signs of depression. She was only partially able to accept the serious nature of the handicap and the poor prognosis, as was seen in her answer to an open question, expressing anxiety lest the boy should not grow up to lead a normal life and be able to work. He had been admitted to hospital at least eight times and usually went into hospital once or twice a year for dilatation of his urethra. She made the comment that she had kept her worries to herself, as she felt that she would 'rather carry it myself than have him (the father) worried'. This mother also had sub-standard housing accommodation, which was an added strain.

Moreover, another deep source of anxiety was recorded in the interview. The mother had had high blood pressure during her pregnancy and was admitted to hospital at the eighth month because of 'kidney trouble', and labour was induced. When the child was admitted to hospital at four months with 'general weakness' (marasmus) and 'kidney trouble', she began to worry about the possible connection between her own condition and the child's. (Further details of this case have been given, p. 47, to illustrate delay in establishing diagnosis.)

A Severe Degree of Over-Anxiety (Case 5)

The child in this case had a severe athetoid paraplegia. The mother complained of anxiety, tension and insomnia, and said that both she and

97

Handicap

her husband were having difficulty in coping now that the child was older and had to be carried everywhere. The parents scored five points for over-anxiety and two points indicating rejection. These were: (i) the mother stated that the child had made the marriage relationship worse because she had had to give too much attention to him; (ii) she had felt ashamed and embarrassed that people should know about his handicap. Marital relations did appear to be strained; the father worked on permanent night-shift. Since the termination of the survey, relations have apparently deteriorated further and the parents are now said not to be on speaking terms.

The child was referred to the Problem Cases Conference for child guidance by the school doctor because he had appeared unhappy and anxious and there were some vomiting episodes. These were subsequently diagnosed as due to an oesophageal stricture, and the child guidance clinic was of the opinion that his difficulties in settling at school were now resolved. The child was severely handicapped and with a marked speech defect but regular treatment was not considered necessary. In any case, the speech defect would have made psychiatric treatment extremely difficult. The teacher's comment was: 'Finds great difficulty in performing usual school functions. Great efforts have been made by him to overcome this handicap and strides have been made in the last few months.'

Summary

For over-anxiety, depression and over-protection alone the results as assessed from the eight items in the survey questionnaire, indicate that:

twenty-one of the parents showed *normal* reactions to the handicap (scores of 0–1);
six showed a *slight* degree of over-anxiety relative to the handicap (scores of 2);
thirteen a *moderately severe* degree of over-anxiety (scores of 3–4);
ten showed *severe* over-anxiety (scores of 5 and over).

Since both aspects of anxiety, the rejecting and the over-protecting, tend to present together, the results were taken together to give a combined score of twelve points (eight for over-protection and four for rejection). On this basis, eighteen parents showed *normal* reactions, four showed a *slight* degree of over-anxiety, fourteen a *moderately* severe degree of over-anxiety and fourteen *severe* over-anxiety.

Thus twenty-eight out of fifty parents, or 56 per cent, experienced moderately severe degrees of over-anxiety and failure to adjust.

Some of the factors predisposing to over-anxiety and adversely affecting emotional adjustment to the handicap, in both children and parents, are considered in Chapters 8 and 9.

EMOTIONAL STRAIN IN THE SIBLINGS

The presence of a handicapped child in a family affects all the members of that family, not only the parents. If the handicapped child gets the extra care, time and attention he needs, correspondingly less can be given the other children. Natural jealousies become intensified, and the handicapped child may be resented by siblings who see him as 'the favourite'.

The siblings' whole social life may have to be adjusted to the handicapped child. They may not be allowed, or may not want, to have their friends in to play. This is particularly likely if their brother or sister is delicate, has embarrassing symptoms, looks odd, or is likely to interfere with play. Family holidays and leisure facilities will be determined by the requirements of the handicapped child, and financial problems (the cost of hospital visits, special footwear, and so on) may add to family resentments.

If family relationships are good, and the mother is able to meet the needs of her handicapped child and still have time for her other children, the siblings are more likely to develop a friendly protective attitude and be more accepting of the limitations imposed by the handicap.

To assess the degree of failure to adjust on the part of the siblings, seven questions were asked about relationships with the handicapped brother or sister.

Out of seven signs of failure to adjust on the part of siblings:

scores of 0–1 were considered to indicate *normal* reactions;
scores of 2 were considered to indicate a *slight* degree of failure to adjust (i.e. within normal limits relative to the handicap);
scores of 3 were considered to indicate a *moderately severe* degree of failure to adjust;
scores of 4 and over were considered to indicate a *severe* degree of failure to adjust.

In thirteen families the handicapped child was an only child. The questions and answers for the remaining thirty-seven families are shown in Appendix V.

WITHDRAWN   99

Handicap

It was clear that many of the mothers were aware of the difficulties of their normal children, and six of the thirty-seven (approximately 16 per cent) readily acknowledged this in answer to Questions 119 and 120. Thirteen mothers (approximately 35 per cent) recognized signs of jealousy or neurotic symptoms. Five mothers thought they neglected their normal children for the handicapped child 'in some ways', though no mother acknowledged 'a great deal' of neglect. Only one considered that she neglected the handicapped child for the normal one. This mother (Case 1) has already been quoted as suffering from moderately severe anxiety and feelings of guilt, associated with the delayed treatment of a urethral stricture and a poor prognosis for the ensuing bilateral hydronephrosis. To Question 123, six mothers (16 per cent) described the attitude of the siblings to the handicapped child as openly hostile and jealous. Some examples follow.

Normal Reaction in Siblings (Case 48)

In this case, Francis, aged nine, suffered from a very troublesome epispadias, which had persisted in spite of five attempts to repair and reconstitute the urethra. In consequence, he had dribbling incontinence, which proved an embarrassment to his siblings. His mother in fact admitted (Question 107) that she still sometimes felt ashamed and embarrassed that people should know about the condition, and that neighbours used to be, and still were, unkind and critical of the child. However, she expressly excluded 'relations' from this category.

There were two older children aged fifteen and seventeen, one of whom was working, and two younger, one of seven and a baby of fourteen months. The mother was in poor health and was under the supervision of a chest clinic. She suffered from breathlessness and lived up five flights of stairs in a big block of flats without a lift. She obviously found it difficult to talk about her embarrassment at having to wash the boy's clothes continually. She appeared, however, to brush aside difficulties as far as the siblings were concerned, though without much conviction. The child himself was described by his mother as 'very helpful and considerate. Manages very well now, but he used to worry and fret.'

A Slight Degree of Failure to Adjust (Case 50)

Edwin, aged seven and a half years, had been left with severe paralysis of the right leg following poliomyelitis when he was three years old. His sister was two years younger, and the mother stated that the sister showed 'marked jealousy' towards him (Question 122) and that her attitude was 'spiteful' (Question 123).

The mother was scored as suffering from moderately severe anxiety, which had somewhat improved since she took a part-time job a year before the interview. The caseworker's comment was: 'Mother is very anxious, and both children are out of hand. There is marked sibling jealousy.'

A Moderately Severe Degree of Failure to Adjust (Case 47)

This was a tragic family in which two boys had severe and progressive muscular dystrophy. The older boy, Chris, aged six years and nine months at the time of the interview, had severe temper tantrums and was referred for child guidance before coming to school. The younger child, Harry, was only two at the time and not yet at school. There was one sister, the oldest child, then eight years old, who was considered by the clinic 'too good and compliant'.

The mother's answers to questions on sibling reactions referred mainly to the two brothers. To Questions 119 and 120 she said that Chris's presence impeded Harry's play and interfered with both siblings' social relationships. She went on to say that although Chris 'idolized' his brother, he sometimes ill-treated him during his tantrums. In fact, shortly before the interview the older child, during an outburst of temper, had actually broken his younger brother's femur by struggling with him in his cot. The mother felt this was a 'terrible thing' and was considering residential placement as a temporary measure.

Many of the difficulties in this family stemmed from the attitude of a robust, athletic father who appeared unable to appreciate the severity of Chris's handicap, resented his disabilities and frequently chastised him. Chris himself, of all the children studied, had the highest score for anxiety. His mother was scored as moderately anxious, showing a slight degree of rejection. The moderately severe degree of sibling anxiety recorded was, perhaps, rather a general expression of the deep-rooted anxieties and conflicts affecting the whole family. (This case is discussed again in Chapter 10 with reference to child guidance.)

A Severe Degree of Failure to Adjust (Case 41)

Hughie was seven years old at the time of the survey. He had a severe congenital heart lesion, for which he had had a Blalock operation at three years. He had shown improvement after this and the question of further operative treatment was continually under review. Owing to various additional anatomical abnormalities, the outcome was viewed with anxiety and the parents were advised that further operative treatment should be indefinitely postponed.

The mother found this advice exceedingly hard to accept, even when a second opinion had confirmed it. She was exceedingly anxious and depressed. A complicating factor was that Hughie suffered from 'epileptic episodes' associated with but not directly due to the cardiac lesion, which the mother believed to be 'heart attacks'. He also suffered, at times, from severe encopresis and enuresis, although this was less marked in school.

This situation affected the siblings, of whom there were four; three older sisters and a younger brother aged three. The mother considered that Hughie's handicap impeded the other children in their play and interfered with their social relationships because of the 'soiling'. She said the youngest child, in particular, showed marked signs of jealousy. Hughie himself tended to ill-treat his younger brother, and the mother thought she had neglected the siblings for her handicapped child 'when he was young'. The thirteen-year-old sister, Nancy, was 'irritable and depressed'. The youngest child, Stephen, was so difficult and demanding, and quarrelled so incessantly with his delicate older brother, that arrangements had been made to get him into a day nursery when four years old.

Sibling anxiety here appeared related to the anxiety, guilt and depression which emanated from the mother and was reflected in the anxieties of the handicapped child. The mother was scored as suffering from severe anxiety, as was the child. The severe sibling anxiety was clearly part of the acute anxiety that permeated the whole family and centred on the handicapped child. (This case also is referred to in Chapter 10, since Hughie attended the psychiatric department of a children's hospital for maladjustment from time to time.)

Summary

Of the thirty-seven families assessed for sibling adjustment:

in twenty-four cases the siblings showed *normal* reactions towards the handicapped child;
in five families a *slight* degree of failure to adjust;
in four instances a *moderately severe* degree of failure to adjust;
in four cases a *severe* degree of failure to adjust.

The results indicate that *in eight of the thirty-seven cases, or over 21 per cent, there was a moderate or severe degree of failure to adjust on the part of the siblings.* It is also apparent from the cases quoted that these figures tend to underestimate the extent of the problem.

The four cases of severe failure to adjust were among the five in which the mother said that she thought she neglected the siblings for the handicapped child. In two of these cases, where there was only one sibling, the children were exceptionally 'difficult' and in need of psychiatric help. In the other two, where there were several children, the siblings appeared to resent the handicapped child quite strongly, but were themselves much less affected.

CHAPTER 8

Factors Affecting the Emotional
Adjustment of the Handicapped Child

DURING the course of the survey it became possible to identify a number of factors tending to increase emotional tensions and anxieties in the child and in some cases to result in his failure to adjust. These factors are now considered.

There are, of course, many interacting influences bearing upon a handicapped child's ability to make a satisfactory adjustment. Among these, two of the most decisive and obvious are the severity of the handicap and the prognosis. Both affect the extent and quality of the mother's anxiety, the element of rejection within that anxiety, and the overall level of stress imposed on the child and his family. Equally important in the outcome are the nature and quality of the family relationships, particularly the marital relationship. Because of his increased dependency these relationships affect a handicapped child even more than they do a normal child.

An additional factor affecting the child's adjustment may be the number and frequency of the child's admissions to hospital. The effects of hospitalization are more difficult to evaluate in a handicapped than in a normal child, and because most handicapped children are admitted to hospital not once but repeatedly, or for prolonged periods, the child's reactions depend to a considerable extent on the individual hospital, the distance from home, the visiting rules and so on.

George (Case 11), whose case has already been given in detail in Chapter 5, illustrates the problems well. He was the child with severe haemophilia and poliomyelitis, whose family moved to a new housing estate outside London. The children's ward in the London hospital to which hitherto he had been admitted for haemorrhages was to him a 'home from home'. It was near his home, he was well known to the staff and greeted as an old friend on his frequent admissions—and his mother could visit easily, leaving the younger children with relatives who lived in the same house. When the family moved, however, the nearest hospital with children's wards was one and a half hours and three separate bus journeys away. It was a big, old-fashioned, gloomy-looking building and the whole atmosphere was much more formal and less well attuned to the special needs of children. The distance, the fares and the difficulty of getting younger children 'minded' in a strange neighbourhood led inevitably to infrequent visits. The child's attitude to hospital changed completely. Visiting days became extremely painful for both the parents and the child, who cried bitterly and begged to be taken home at every visit.

In an attempt to assess the various components in the children's emotional problems, the following factors were considered:

   (i) the severity of the handicap;
  (ii) the prognosis;
 (iii) parental reactions (if rejection, whether open or masked);
 (iv) marital relations (when known);
  (v) hospitalization (number and duration of hospital admissions).

It was not always possible for the interviewer to make an assessment of parental reactions and relationships at the survey interview unless the family situation was already known, and the difficulties increased with elements of rejection or ambivalence in the mother's responses. In every case, therefore, discussions with the caseworker and information from records were also used.

Tables A, B, C and D in Appendix VIII record these factors as assessed at the survey interviews, from the records and from selected responses to the two questionnaires (see Chapters 6 and 7). They indicate whether the mother's anxieties and attitudes of rejection could be regarded as masked or open; record the nature of the marital relationship, where known; and offer some general comments on individual cases. Although parental reactions are referred to, in most cases it was the mother who was seen at the survey interview and it is therefore her comments which are most often recorded. For the purposes of these tables normal and slight emotional difficulties are grouped together, as are moderately severe and severe emotional difficulties in the parents and children, to present an assessment of the factors affecting the emotional adjustment of both parents and child, grouped according to their similar or differing reactions.

Handicap

TABLE A: NORMAL OR SLIGHT EMOTIONAL DIFFICULTIES IN
BOTH THE CHILD AND THE PARENTS

Table A includes twelve cases under this heading.

Severity of the Handicap

The handicaps in this group were slight in seven cases, moderate in three, and severe in two. Three of the cases with a slight handicap were children with poliomyelitis involving one leg. A fourth case of poliomyelitis was assessed as a moderate handicap since it involved the right arm and shoulder girdle.

Prognosis

In the two cases in which the handicap was severe the prognosis was poor in one and fair in the other. In Case 46, with the poor prognosis, the child with severe haemophilia had been adopted and was eleven months old before the condition was discovered. The adoptive mother's anxiety, assessed as slight, appeared to derive from her own indifferent health and recent operations, and perhaps from the responsibilities she had undertaken, rather than from the child's handicap. Her anxieties appeared objective, in contrast to the mothers of the three other children with haemophilia in the survey, who suffered from severely subjective feelings of guilt and anxiety. In the second case (26), although the handicap was severe there was little cause for anxiety for the child's life, and a 'fair' prognosis in relation to normal achievement.

Parental Reactions: Rejection masked

There were two cases (4 and 29) in which parental rejection was scored and this appeared well masked in both.

Case 4, the boy with paralysis of his right arm and shoulder girdle, revealed an odd history of two fires in the home: one in which his sound hand was severely burned, and a second in which the house was largely destroyed. His mother repeated three times during the interview her fears that the boy would feel 'inferior' and 'unable to do things'. She added that he was 'too quiet' and that he frequently remarked. 'If only I had both arms'. She also asked how she could persuade him to use his paralysed arm a little rather than ignore it. Her attitude suggested some feelings of guilt and rejection towards this boy, who was the first child of her second marriage. Her answers to the questionnaire, however, resulted in a score indicating a normal reaction for herself and slight anxiety for the boy.

The other case in this group in which anxiety was notably marked was that of the little girl with achondroplasia (dwarfism). The mother was able to admit her outright rejection of the infant during the first six weeks, but she found it impossible to acknowledge her continuing feelings of guilt, anxiety and partial rejection at the interview.

Parental Reactions: Rejection—open

Open rejection was recorded in the questionnaire in the following six cases, in addition to the cases of masked rejection described above.

In Case 7, first the father and then the mother deserted, and the child was brought up by grandparents.

In Case 29 (a girl with mild poliomyelitis affecting one leg), the mother had deserted the family while Naomi was in hospital. Although there were no signs of rejection by the father, Naomi had shown some signs of anxiety and deprivation, with mild pilfering, when she first returned to school.

In Case 8, Charlie had been in hospital for almost four years with a tuberculous spine, as he was not allowed home until the family found better accommodation. Furthermore, the parents were said by his teacher to take little or no interest in his education.

In Case 40 (a boy with mild poliomyelitis involving one leg), the medical records noted that Oliver was 'rather nervy and isolated at home, following the advent of a new baby'. The teachers' questionnaire scored one point for rejection, with the remark: 'He has fits of obstinacy, when he refuses to say a word—even though he may be praised.' At the survey interview, in answer to the final question asking what she would do differently 'if she had it all to do over again', the mother said that she would 'give more time and patience and try to understand' the handicapped child.

There were somewhat similar indications of rejection in Case 43, another boy with mild poliomyelitis involving one leg. His mother had visited him in hospital only when his sister was also admitted with poliomyelitis. His father had suffered from acute anxiety and insomnia during the six months that both children were in hospital and had continued to visit weekly, but alone, for the remainder of the twenty-two months that Noel was in hospital, after his sister's return home. Although the child

Handicap

was said to have been extremely anxious when he first came out of hospital, and was terrified of buses, noises, fire and so on, his fears wore off gradually and he was assessed as only 'slightly anxious'.

In Case 46 (severe haemophilia), the child had been handed over to the adoptive parents at eight days old (initial maternal rejection).

Marital Relations

In two cases marital relations were noted as poor and broken, respectively. These were both cases in which there was open rejection. In the first (Case 8), the child appeared withdrawn and little affection was evident, and in the second (Case 29), although there were initial emotional difficulties following the mother's desertion, the father's continued care and affection appeared to provide at least current stability.

Hospitalization

The number of hospital admissions varied from none to twenty-six and the duration in weeks from nought to 200. It proved impossible to assess the effects of hospitalization in each child, as a factor in isolation.

Summary

There was considerable variation in most factors: the handicap varied from slight to severe and the prognosis from good to poor. The number of hospital admissions varied from none to twenty-six and the duration from nil to 200 weeks.

The key factor in every case appeared to be the attitude of the parents. Where the mother showed only slight or normal indications of emotional difficulties the child's attitude was the same, even when the handicap was severe and the prognosis poor, as in the case of the adoptive parents of the child with severe haemophilia. In three cases this factor was expressed in the doctor's comment after the interview: 'The mother appears well adjusted.'

On the other hand, where the parents' attitude was one of open or masked rejection (in eight cases out of the twelve) the comments column records some indications of anxiety or withdrawal on the part of seven of the children. These appear, however, to have been sufficiently well disguised to evade the mother's recognition in her answers to the questionnaire. The eighth child, initially rejected at adoption, was *not* rejected by his adoptive parents.

TABLE B: NORMAL OR SLIGHT EMOTIONAL DIFFICULTIES IN
THE CHILD; MODERATELY SEVERE OR SEVERE IN THE PARENTS

Table B includes ten cases under this heading. The factors are summarized as before, and appear at the foot of Table B.

As might be expected, the significant factor in the mothers' more intense emotional problems appears to be the number of poor or broken marital relations, seven out of the ten cases. In the other three, little was known of the marital relationships, but in one of these (Case 1) the mother suffered from marked feelings of guilt and depression, which she said she'd 'rather carry herself than have the father worried'. In Case 36 the mother suffered from agoraphobia and there was a history of the loss of her first two children, one at three months and the second stillborn.

In Case 48 (epispadias), the mother's admission of shame and embarrassment about the child's handicap was clearly connected with feelings of guilt and rejection, and the child's emotional difficulties appeared suppressed.

The children on the other hand appeared relatively free from emotional complications, although again there was some indication of difficulties in adjustment, recorded in the comments column. This may have been due in part to the fact that of the seven instances of open rejection, four involved the father only, and the mothers in this group were exceptionally devoted.

TABLE C: MODERATELY SEVERE OR SEVERE EMOTIONAL DIFFICULTIES
IN THE CHILD; NORMAL OR SLIGHT IN THE PARENTS

Table C includes ten cases under this heading.

Severity of the Handicap

The handicap was slight in six cases, moderate in one and severe in three. Of these three, two were cases of severe cerebral palsy, the third was a case of muscular dystrophy. The moderately severe handicap was also a case of cerebral palsy.

Four of the children with slight handicaps had mild degrees of cerebral palsy: the remaining two had, respectively, mild epilepsy and a bilateral talipes.

Handicap

Prognosis

In two cases the prognosis was poor in relation to life; in six, good in relation to life but only fair in relation to normal attainments (listed as fair); and in two it was good in both respects.

Parental Reactions

In one of the cases (Case 30) in which the prognosis was poor, the child had muscular dystrophy. Her brother (previously at the school) had a similar condition, and her mother was thought to have died from it. The children were looked after by their father and an aunt, herself suffering from chronic tuberculosis and caring for an invalid mother. The atmosphere appeared surprisingly normal and cheerful, and there were no obvious signs of failure to adjust to what most people would clearly have found an almost intolerable burden. The child herself was said to have been very upset for some months after her mother's death, and 'couldn't bear to be left alone'.

In Case 33, the delicate child with cerebral palsy where the prognosis was also poor, the mother's expressed anxieties were in relation to very poor housing conditions, and the distance she had to take the child to hospital. She appeared unable to admit her anxiety about the child directly. The child, however, appeared nervous and timid and afraid of the dark.

In this group also the key factor in the child's adjustment appeared to be the parents' attitude. With all these children showing moderate or severe signs of inability to adjust to their handicap, rejection was either open or masked in every case (see comments). In six cases it was open, including one maternal death and two cases of desertion by one or both parents. In Case 2, the child was rejected by the whole family, and especially the grandparents, because his handicap had resulted in the refusal of an eagerly awaited emigration permit. In Case 21, the parents were at first unable to accept the child's retardation, although their attitudes later improved as a result of consistent home visiting by a psychiatric social worker.

Case 33 has already been quoted in relation to the poor prognosis, and the mother's inability to face her anxieties in relation to the child.

There were, in addition, four cases in which rejection appeared to be masked.

In Case 17, a child with cerebral ataxia due to neo-natal anoxia, the mother expressed her anxiety about the cause of the handicap and delay in diagnosis. She was also looking forward to a move to new accommodation where there would be a cousin of eleven, who would help look after the child. It was clear that she was finding it difficult to cope herself.

In Case 18, another spastic hemiplegia following a difficult birth, the mother felt quite unable to face another pregnancy, although both parents were aware that Stuart was very much of an only child.

In Case 25, a mild case of epilepsy, the mother appeared unable to accept the associated mental retardation and had had a breakdown.

In Case 44, a mild spastic paraplegia, the mother appeared not only to ignore the child's handicap, but the child himself, leaving him mainly to the care of his grandmother and frequently missing his appointments for treatment.

Marital Relations

These were noted in only three out of the ten cases and were poor in two, broken in a third.

Hospitalization

Admissions varied from none to twenty-two, with durations from nil to forty-five weeks. Again it appeared impossible to assess the child's reactions to this factor in isolation.

Summary

In this group of children showing moderate or severe difficulties in adjusting to their handicaps, the main factor again appeared to be the attitude of the parents, and in particular the attitude of rejection whether open or masked. The fact that this appeared in every case in this group perhaps accounts for the moderately severe or severe emotional problems of all the children, and for the less obvious degree of emotional difficulties in the parents.

TABLE D: MODERATELY SEVERE OR SEVERE EMOTIONAL DIFFICULTIES
IN BOTH THE CHILD AND THE PARENTS

Table D includes twelve cases in which both children and parents suffered from moderately severe or severe emotional difficulties. The combination of adverse factors here, the severity of the handicap, the poor prognosis and the poor or broken marital relations appear inter-related, and in only one case (45) were none of these factors present. In this case the mother was suffering from severe agoraphobia and had been under the psychiatric department of a hospital for three years. The child suffered from fears of the dark, temper tantrums and aggressive behaviour.

Eight of the twelve children had severe defects, and two moderately severe. The prognosis in five was poor, in six fair.

The number of children scored for rejection was nine; in six cases this was considered open rejection, and in three others masked.

Marital relations were poor or broken in seven cases, and in one the mother was a widow.

TABLE E: MODERATELY SEVERE OR SEVERE EMOTIONAL DIFFICULTIES
IN THE CHILD, THE PARENTS AND THE SIBLINGS

The final table shows six cases of moderately severe or severe emotional problems in the whole family: parents, handicapped child and siblings. All the children had severe or moderately severe handicaps, the prognosis was poor in four, and only fair in the other two. Rejection was open in five of the six cases, and considered masked in the sixth. Marital relations were broken or poor in three of the six cases.

DISCUSSION

Parental reactions, as might be expected, were found to be the key factor in determining the extent of the child's emotional difficulties. It became clear, moreover, that where there was an element of rejection, the effect was still more marked.

The nature of rejection within the parent-child relationship showed great variation in both cause and effect. Some of these causes became apparent from the case histories. In one case the child's handicap had put an end to the family's hopes of emigration; in another, an athletic father was deeply disappointed in having a handicapped son. In other cases open rejection was seen in the break-up of the family and the father's 'desertion', although the presence of a handicapped child may or may not have been decisive in the breakdown of marital relations. In general, the presence of a severe handicap, or of a handicap with a fatal prognosis, can be so difficult and painful to accept that the parents—more often the mother, who feels especially responsible—are quite unable to come to terms with it in a realistic way. If the parents are unable to accept the handicap and to make the necessary adjustments, the child may feel that they cannot accept him, and will feel rejected.

Of all the painful emotions associated with a handicap perhaps the most severe are felt by the mothers, who believe they are guilty or at fault. Whether these feelings are based on fact or fantasy, the sense of guilt can cause so much distress that they can react only by rejecting the cause —the child himself. This conflict may be expressed in the ambivalent feelings of parents towards the handicapped child.

Parents can be helped to understand and accept their painful feelings by experienced caseworkers. The greatest emotional difficulties—and, in consequence, the greatest need for skilled help—are likely to occur in those cases where the parents are told that their children will be unlikely to survive adolescence. In nearly half (seven) of the cases in this category in the sample studied, marital relations were strained almost to breaking point, and in two of them there had been temporary separations. The constant anxiety, the feelings of guilt, the tendency for each partner to blame the other if the handicap is congenital, the mother's often exclusive preoccupation with the handicapped child, must all be factors in this situation. In the face of such problems, the wonder is that so many marriages remain intact and are, in fact, strengthened by the sharing of anxieties about the handicapped child.

CHAPTER 9

Factors Affecting the Emotional Adjustment
of the Parents

IT HAS been shown that the degree and quality of parental anxiety are of key significance for the emotional adjustment of the child. We are now concerned to identify the various factors contributing to the parents' anxieties, and to examine how these anxieties affect the family's ability to make a satisfactory adjustment. Some of the sources of parental anxiety have already been discussed in relation to the child—in particular, the severity of the handicap and the prognosis. The implications of these two factors are naturally clearer to the parents than to the child. Other factors relate only to the parents, although the sum total of their anxieties will be reflected in the emotional difficulties of the child.

For purposes of analysis, parental anxieties were grouped as follows:

ANXIETIES RELATING TO THE HANDICAPPED CHILD

(i) the severity of the handicap
(ii) the prognosis
(iii) fears concerning the child's future: employment prospects, family life, etc.
(iv) fears about the ultimate care of the child; the possible need for institutional care.

ANXIETIES RELATING TO THE PARENTS THEMSELVES

(i) fear of future pregnancies, and problems of birth control
(ii) marital disharmonies and separations
(iii) parental ill health: physical and mental
(iv) social conditions.

ANXIETIES RELATING TO THE HANDICAPPED CHILD

The Severity of the Handicap

Twenty-three cases were assessed as severe from the survey questionnaire, ten as moderately severe, and seventeen as slight.

Eighteen of the parents of the twenty-three severely handicapped children were rated as showing moderately severe or severe emotional difficulties.

The Prognosis

In sixteen cases out of the fifty, the medical prognosis was poor. For three of these children there appeared to be little hope of survival to adult life: these were the two children with muscular dystrophy and the child with an inoperable thalamic glioma. Parental reactions to these factors were discussed in the previous chapter.

Thirteen of these appeared in the group of severe and moderately severe parental anxiety.

Fears Concerning the Child's Future

Of the ten parents who answered 'no problem' to Question 53,* four of the children have since gone back to ordinary school, and a fifth is going shortly. The other five have mild disabilities and at least three will probably return to ordinary school later.

The majority of the parents (80 per cent) acknowledged that fears about the child's future were a source of considerable anxiety to them. Their fears centred around questions such as the possibilities of employment, of managing and supporting a home of their own, and of limitations in sport, leisure and other social activities.

Fears of the Child's Ultimate Admission to an Institution

Amongst the worst fears about the child's future was the problem of future care in the event of the parents' death ('What do the parents think will happen to the child in the future if either or both die?')

Of the thirty-three mothers who said 'relatives', two added, rather uncertainly, 'I hope', and four specified, somewhat unrealistically, 'grandparents'. Of the eight parents who said 'institution', five did so

* 'Is the problem of what will happen to him in the future no problem/a major worry/ a cause of family conflict/a worry but solution has been accepted.'

with varying degrees of pain and embarrassment. Eight mothers answered, 'Don't think about it', and two added, 'I *daren't* think about it'. Two of the others were 'young', and said they didn't have to worry. In the fifth case the handicap was slight enough to cause little incapacity.

In the sixth case the prognosis was so grave (Case 12, a Fallot's tetralogy, with heart failure) the mother indicated that she thought it unnecessary to answer since she had been warned that the child was unlikely to survive adolescence. This was one of the most anxious and maladjusted mothers in the whole series.

In the seventh case (Case 33, the delicate little girl with hemiplegia and tuberculosis) the mother was obviously too overwhelmed with immediate problems to have given much thought to the future.

In the eighth case (Case 36, a child with poliomyelitis) the mother was a deeply disturbed and anxious woman. She had lost her first two children, and had felt unable to leave the three others for seven years, except on one occasion when she had been persuaded to go out, but returned in an hour. She was too much preoccupied with her own problems to have given much thought to the future of the handicapped child.

Seven of the others who thought their children would have to go into institutions were in the group of severely or moderately anxious parents. The eighth was in the normal group, and although the mother answered 'institution', the father added, rather lightheartedly: 'Hope she'll be able to look after herself.' This was Rosie, the child (Case 21) with spastic quadriplegia and some brain damage, following tuberculous meningitis, whose parents had at first found great difficulty in accepting her handicap, but had been helped to do so through the weekly visits of a psychiatric social worker from the Invalid Children's Aid Association, over a period of eighteen months. Her father qualified his remark by adding that he was helping the child to buy a doll on hire purchase with her weekly pocket money 'to teach her about money'. She was a pretty child, and father clearly hoped that marriage would be the solution.

ANXIETIES RELATING TO THE PARENTS

Fear of Further Pregnancies and Problems of Birth Control

The fear of future pregnancies, including the fear of having another handicapped child and the burden of trying to look after younger children in addition to the handicapped child, especially where the handicap was severe, was almost universal. These fears were usually expressed only in answer to a specific question. Question 104 asked: 'How did the knowledge that their child was handicapped affect the parents' attitude to having other children?'

Twenty-eight parents expressed their anxieties about future pregnancies, including sixteen who had already decided not to have more children.

Only five mothers who might have been expected to express anxiety about future pregnancies did not do so, and three of these were amongst the mildest handicaps.

TABLE 14
Parents Seeking advice on Birth Control or Genetics

Case		Birth Control (B.C.)	Genetic Counselling	Advice Followed	Further Pregnancies
11	(Haemophilia)	1	1	B.C. Clinic (R.C.)	4 (not intended)
14	(Cerebral tumour)	1	–	B.C. clinic	1 (not intended)
21	(T.B. Meningitis)	1	–	B.C. clinic	0
23	(Achondroplasia)	1	1	Birth control (unspecified)	0
26	(Severely spastic)	1	1 (Rh. factor)	B.C. clinic	(Father's breakdown and mother's ultimate sterilization)
30	(Muscular Dystrophy)	–	1	Hysterectomy	0
31	(Congenital Heart)	–	1	—	1
35	(Severely spastic)	–	1	Cervical tear	0
42	(Haemophilia)	1	1	B.C. clinic	0
43	(Polio)	1	–	Hysterectomy (3rd Caesarean)	0
44	(Mildly spastic)	–	1	Decided to have more	3
47	(Muscular Dystrophy)	1	1	B.C. clinic (R.C.)	1 (not intended)
49	(Haemophilia)	1	1	Hysterectomy	0
		9	10	10	6 pregnancies not intended

Handicap

Approximately eighty per cent of the mothers of children with congenital handicaps expressed their fears of further pregnancies.

Question 106 was worded so as to give some indication of attitudes to both genetics and birth control: 'Did they seek advice whether to have more children?'

Of the forty-one mothers to whom the questions applied, only thirteen replied affirmatively. These are listed in Table 14 and the type of advice received specified. As is also shown, not all advice was followed. Even among those who did attempt to follow instructions, the results were not necessarily successful.

Nine of the mothers ultimately sought birth-control advice, three had hysterectomies, and one decided to have another child.

Three families had children while suffering from feelings of severe anxiety and guilt in relation to the first child. In Case 11, the mother attended the Catholic Marriage Guidance Centre and subsequently had four more pregnancies, all boys, three of them confirmed haemophilics. The burden of anxiety and guilt in addition to the social complications has seriously affected marriage relations which were previously of the happiest.

Additional problems are indicated by the fact that of the ten parents who sought advice and followed it, only six belonged to the group who 'decided not to have any more' children. The remaining ten in that group did not seek birth control advice—nor did they have further pregnancies. They included four families in which severe marital disharmony was recorded. In one case of severe congenital multiple deformities, the mother stated that there had been no marital relations since the birth of the child, and a temporary separation of the parents followed.

Even amongst the group who had sought birth control advice, there were two examples of severe marital disharmony—both cases of haemophilia. In one the mother said she 'would break the marriage, if she did not feel a broken home would be bad for the child'.

In the seven cases in which parents expressed anxiety about another handicapped child being born, only one sought birth control advice (Case 11 referred to above). All had more children (five were Roman Catholics).

In the five who worried about having others because of the handicapped child, only one sought birth control advice, but in each case no further pregnancies occurred.

118

Cases of Sterilization

There were four mothers who had been sterilized (Cases 30, 49, 43 and 13). In two this was directly related to the handicap (Case 30, a muscular dystrophy, and Case 49, a severe haemophilia). In two of the cases (49 and 13) the sterilization was preceded and followed by extreme degrees of marital disharmony.

A fifth sterilization (Case 26, a severe athetoid spastic, due to Rhesus antibodies) followed the termination of the survey, but took place as a result of the three interviews, the preliminary survey, the interview with the full questionnaire and the control interview. The mother wrote later to say that the operation had been successfully carried out, soon after the survey was closed, to her own and her husband's infinite relief.

Marital Disharmonies and Separations

Some of the causes of marital disharmony have already been discussed, but there are others.

Many parents are deeply anxious about the cause of the handicap and many have feelings of guilt based on factors such as chronic alcoholism, problems concerning inadequate birth control, or attempts at abortion.

Others may have less realistic but equally disturbing fears of guilt and retribution, due to minor indiscretions during pregnancy and many other causes.

Question 137 was designed with this in mind: 'Do the parents have any worries or fears about what may have been the cause of the defect?'

Of the twenty-six mothers who said that they had *no* fears or anxieties, nine had children with acquired handicaps, four were haemophilics and two had muscular dystrophy (the parents said they accepted the hereditary nature of the disease). Four accepted the fact that the handicap was due to a difficult confinement; one knew that the handicap was due to rubella in pregnancy. Three said they accepted the handicap without knowing the cause, and three made no comment, although their anxiety was apparent in answers to other questions.

Although the four haemophilic cases are included amongst the 'no worries or fears about . . . the cause of the defect', parental friction and recriminations were recognized in two of the cases which were referred for child guidance.

Of the four who had accepted the fact that the handicap was due to a

Handicap

difficult confinement, two were unable to face further pregnancies although they would have liked other children. The third 'accepted it, but wished "she" had been born in hospital, owing to the lung collapse'. In fact, the baby had been given oxygen for asphyxia, following a home confinement, and the oxygen had run out. When she reached hospital with the baby, the mother was told that one lung had failed to expand. In the fourth case, the cord was round the baby's neck twice and he was born 'white'. There were two further pregnancies before the parents separated. There was clearly considerable anxiety in these cases, although the cause of the handicap was recognized and 'accepted'.

Among the twenty-three who answered that they did have worries or fears were such comments as 'prefers not to know what cause may have been' (Case 24, the severe haemangioma of the face and shoulders. This mother had been treated with radium for a rodent ulcer during the pregnancy though this would not appear to justify her cryptic comment).

The expression 'wonders why', or 'worried how it started', recurs again and again.

To summarize, with the exception of nine cases in which the handicap was acquired, considerable anxiety as to the cause of the handicap appeared to be present in each of the remaining forty-one cases, and in many it was marked.

Separations

Some of the problems associated with rejection of the child by one or both parents have already been discussed. Extreme degrees of rejection are shown in the following table:

Father deserted	Mother deserted	Both deserted
4 (permanently, including one illegitimate)	1 (permanently)	1 (permanently)
3 (temporarily)		

Thus, in nine families (18 per cent) one or both parents deserted the handicapped child, in six permanently and in three temporarily. Five of these ended in divorce, leaving three mothers and one father to bring up the handicapped child alone. In two others the child was brought up by grandparents. These were the extreme cases of complete and permanent rejection, but milder degrees of rejection by either parent have been noted repeatedly. They are a fruitful cause of parental friction and re-crimination, and an obvious indication of failure to adjust to the handicap. In addition, there were two parental deaths, one mother and one father.

Quarrels about the Child

Difficulties can also arise where either parent (usually the mother) is over-anxious and over-protective, and the other spouse (usually the father) blames the mother for her handling of the child. In answer to Question 102, 'Are there frequent quarrels between mother and father?', seven mothers *admitted* quarrelling about the child, and eight about other matters, usually financial (two about both).

The records of the interviews indicated a considerable element of doubt about this question. Few parents are inclined to acknowledge dis-agreements over the handling of children. It is natural to suppose that these disagreements would be more emotionally charged, and hence more difficult to admit, in the case of handicapped children. It was clear that in answer to the direct question disagreements amounting to quarrels were often denied; but they were often indirectly acknowledged in other answers.

The question of holiday and leisure facilities for the handicapped child and the family are discussed in the social section. The main difficulty is that parents can seldom go out together and the father must pursue his interests alone.

Fourteen fathers did not go out for recreation without the child whereas twenty-eight reported going out at least once a week without the child.

The same applied to holidays. Among the 50 per cent of families who said their holidays were 'complicated' by the child's handicap, the restrictions as to place and accommodation chosen appeared to fall most heavily on the fathers, whose holidays had always to be geared to the needs of the handicapped child.

It was obvious that, for the most part, fathers took a considerable part in the care of their handicapped children, as was revealed by Question 43: 'What does father do as his share of caring for the child when the child is at home?'

The answers revealed that twenty-one shared completely in minding and occupying him and seventeen spent their time with him when free. Three looked after him when mother was out and one helped occa-sionally.

Only six did nothing, and of these four were amongst those who ultimately deserted, and one was a chronic alcoholic who had never looked after his other children. The sixth father had taken no part in caring for the child because 'mother would not let him'.

The final question in this series was: 'How has the child affected the marriage relationship? Illustrate.' The mothers naturally took some time to think about this unexpected question. The figures for their rather hastily considered answers are given below:

Improved it	10
Had no effect	33
Made it worse	6
Not applicable	1
	—
	50

The ten mothers who said 'improved it', typically made a comment such as: 'has drawn us closer together—sharing each other's anxiety.'

Of the thirty-three who said 'no effect', four implied 'it couldn't be worse'.

Of the six who said 'made it worse', two fathers had deserted, and the other couples were having marital difficulties. One father had left home temporarily, one was on permanent night-shift, and in one case the mother said she would have left her husband if she hadn't felt a broken home would be bad for the child.

PARENTAL HEALTH: PHYSICAL

Poor health in any member of the family, particularly the mother, adds to the strain on any family with a handicapped child.

Questions 70 and 71 dealt with this problem and the answers showed that twenty-one near relatives were under a hospital or their own doctor for various conditions. In seven of the nine cases where father was ill, both parents were under hospital or their own doctor, and two siblings were under child guidance.

The sum total of illness in these families appears overwhelming, and in fact, four of them were in the 'severely anxious' group.

Mother's Health: Physical

This was considered separately because of its importance for the handicapped child (Question 72).

Twenty-four mothers reported suffering from a chronic illness or physical disability. On closer questioning, however (Question 79: 'Other notes about mother (Prompt—menorrhagia, etc.)') another fourteen mothers answered that they were suffering from various complaints such as menorrhagia or other gynaecological conditions, anxiety and excessive fatigue, and chronic bronchitis.

The total number of mothers suffering from chronic illness or physical disability may therefore be closer to 76 per cent.

PARENTAL HEALTH: MENTAL

The nervous strain on other members of a family with a handicapped child is obviously considerable. In answer to Question 71: 'Is mother concerned about the health or behaviour of any other member of the household ?', the following figures resulted.

Fathers

four fathers were suffering from anxiety states of varying degrees,
two from acute anxiety states (hospital treatment),
one from chronic anxiety and duodenal ulcer (doctor treating),
one from chronic alcoholism (previous to child's handicap).
(Apart from the father with chronic alcoholism, the other conditions appeared to be directly related to the child's handicap.)

Siblings

eight siblings were suffering from mental or emotional conditions,
three showed marked signs of maladjustment,
one showed marked signs of anxiety, and attended C.G.C.,
one suffered from severe enuresis, and attended a special investigation
    clinic,
one suffered from fits,
one suffered from infantile eczema,
one was an imbecile.
(Five of these conditions appeared to be directly related to the handicapped child.)

Mother

A series of six questions (73–78) related to the mother's mental health. Summarizing the answers:

thirteen mothers were frequently or always very depressed
thirty-two sometimes felt everything was too much and they couldn't cope
fifteen worried so much they couldn't sleep
eighteen could never relax, and always had to be 'on the go'
seventeen suffered from frequent headaches
eighteen always felt tired and run down

Taking these figures together:

7 mothers suffered from 5 symptoms
6   "   "   " 4 "
7   "   "   " 3 "
5   "   "   " 2 "
8   "   "   " 1 "
—
33   1 or more symptoms

Thus almost two-thirds of the mothers suffered from varying degrees of anxiety, depression, tension or fatigue directly related to the handicapped child. Additional comments from the mothers themselves, in answer to an open question, appeared to confirm these figures: thirty complained directly of 'depression and anxiety', 'bad nerves', 'fatigue and depression', 'harassed and tired', 'just worry', or similar comments. Eight were among those attending child guidance clinics, two were attending hospital and two a psychiatrist. The remainder were attending their own doctors from time to time.

SOCIAL CONDITIONS

While social conditions are unlikely to be the determining factor in the success or failure of a family in adjusting to the needs of a handicapped child, they clearly play an important part.

The most striking example of the importance of social conditions in the broadest sense was the deterioration in morale of the family who moved out of London to the new housing estate (Case 11). The absence of social amenities and the loss of the higher standard of social services previously available proved a much greater obstacle to adjustment than a damp and overcrowded basement. The case has already been described in detail in Chapter 5.

It is only fair to add that had there been no further pregnancies (or at least no more children with haemophilia) the deterioration in marital relations would probably have been less marked. But for the child with haemophilia and poliomyelitis, the absence of a day school for the physically handicapped, and the distance from hospitals and clinics, could have been little short of disastrous whatever else the circumstances.

In Case 10, in which the family was unable to find suitable housing accommodation in London and returned to Wales, the absence of a day school for the physically handicapped necessitated the child's admission to a boarding school. In this case, however, the child was older, and the family already broken by the father's desertion. Both mother and child accepted the situation quite readily.

Apart from the lower standard or absence of some of the social services outside London, the effects of social conditions on the families with a handicapped child could be seen most clearly in their housing conditions. The examples in Chapter 5 could be multiplied endlessly, but perhaps only two further illustrations will suffice.

In Case 33, a family of five was living in two tiny rooms on the top floor of a small house, with a stove on the landing for a kitchen. The outside lavatory was shared with ten other people. The handicapped child was suffering from cerebral palsy with mild athetosis. At the interview, Mandy was seven years old, but in very poor health following bronchitis with a collapsed lung the year before. This was followed by bronchietasis, and finally, pulmonary tuberculosis. At the interview she was found to be sleeping on a chairbed in the sitting-room, where her parents also had to sleep on a Put-U-Up. The two older children, a boy of nine and a girl of twelve, had Put-U-Up beds in the tiny room next door which had to be taken down each day to let them move about the room. We could at last understand why all the persuasive arguments about early bed for a sick child had apparently fallen on deaf ears.

The doctor's assessment immediately after the interview was, 'Mother depressed, tired; cannot cope, considers child coping with disability, but not with ill health.' Mother herself said she was 'depressed—no room to put anything.' Great efforts were made and the family was rehoused in a council flat three months later. There was an almost immediate improvement in the health and morale of mother and child, and consequently in their ability to bear the burden of the child's handicap.

The other case has also been mentioned above (Case 46). The adoptive mother of the child with severe haemophilia was so concerned with her housing problem, and its effect on her own and the child's health, that this appeared to overshadow all other anxieties. She lived with her husband and child in four rooms, on two floors at the top of a house, up fifty-seven steps. The stairs were covered with rather slippery linoleum and the banisters were rickety and unsafe.

The child had fallen on several occasions, and just previous to the interview had a haemorrhage into the knee joint and was wearing a hip caliper. He had, therefore, to be carried up and down fifty-seven steps or else be allowed to take a very long time, with risks of further injury. His father, a van driver, was usually at work when John was due for the school bus, and when he arrived home at about four o'clock. His mother had been operated on for a ruptured ovarian cyst several years previously, and been advised against lifting. In any case she found the strain of carrying a six-year-old boy with a hip caliper up and down fifty-seven stairs every day almost intolerable. Since the flat was on two floors, she had also to carry or support the boy when he went to the kitchen for meals or to the toilet. She was in constant fear of further falls. This family was rehoused about a year later, on medical grounds.

Apart from housing, financial difficulties sometimes hampered the possibility of satisfactory adjustment.

In Case 15, for example, the teachers' questionnaire recorded a moderate degree of rejection by the parents, and the school doctor referred to the mother's depression and anxiety. Father was a lorry driver earning about £8 a week, and there were five children under ten. To supplement their family allowances, mother took odd jobs, but as there were two children under school age, this was not easy. Her rent was £1 18s. 5d. She complained of the expenses of visiting the child in hospital about fifteen miles outside London for fifty-six weeks in all. She was also continually in financial difficulties with his boots, which needed repairing every three weeks, and with the expense of reporting back to the hospital after his discharge every few months. The family were unable to afford holidays, and the only play space available was the dirty backyard of the big block of flats where they lived. Even here there were coal lorries and vans continually unloading and turning, adding to her anxieties for the child, who was on crutches.

In Case 24, there were also five children. The father, who was an un-skilled builder's labourer, had been off work for eleven months with three operations. They lived in a dilapidated house in a rough and noisy neigh-bourhood, next to a bomb site used as a playground by the local children. The child with a large and grossly disfiguring haemangioma involving her face, head and thorax, had had an intra-cranial haemorrhage at four months, causing a partial hemiplegia and fits. She suffered from severe temper tantrums and other behaviour problems.

Had this family lived in a small house or flat with a garden, the child's disfigurement might have provoked less comment, resentment and retalia-tion, and the child become less aggressive and subject to her severe temper tantrums.

SIBLINGS

In the eight cases where siblings showed severe signs of failure to adjust, there were a number of common factors, already discussed (see page 102).

The handicap was severe in six cases and moderately severe in two, including the child with spastic diplegia, dysarthria, and encopresis (Case 6). In her case and in two other cases of cerebral palsy, the outlook was fair in relation to survival but poor in relation to normal attainment. In the other five cases the prognosis was poor in relation to both survival and normal attainment.

Maternal anxiety, as might be expected, was severe in five cases and moderately severe in two cases. The eighth case, in which maternal anxiety is recorded as normal, was an outstanding example of acceptance and adjustment on the part of the mother. The father, on the other hand, had been admitted to a neurological hospital for investigation, and suffered a serious breakdown which was attributed to the strains associated with the handicapped child; the child's sister also showed signs of failure to adjust to the situation.

Similarly, in five out of eight cases the handicapped child's own anxiety was severe and in one, moderately severe. In the seventh, the child was mentally retarded and thus incapable of fully appreciating the position. The eighth was the case quoted above, where the mother and child had made a good adjustment to a very severe handicap.

Thus the main factors affecting sibling difficulties in emotional adjust-ment appeared to be the severity of the handicap, the extent of maternal anxiety and the handicapped child's own emotional difficulties.

Handicap

TABLE 13
Factors Affecting Sibling Adjustment

Case No.	Severity of Handicap	Prognosis	Maternal Anxiety	Handicapped Child's Anxiety	Comments
6	Moderately Severe	Fair	Severe	Severe	Child guidance considered; not accepted
14	Severe	Poor (fatal)	Severe	Moderately severe	Child only 5 yr. old
24	Severe	Poor	Severe	Severe	Child under hospital psychiatrist
41	Severe	Poor	Severe	Severe	Child under hospital psychiatrist
19	Severe	Poor	Severe	Slight	Child severely retarded
26	Severe	Fair	Normal	Slight	Good adjustment
32	Moderately Severe	Fair	Severe	Severe	Mother had frequent asthmatic attacks
47	Severe	Poor (fatal)	Moderate	Severe	Under child guidance

CHAPTER 10

Treatment, Supervision and Support

Forms of Advice and Guidance Given for Psychological Problems in a Small School

THE FORMS of advice given in the school which was the subject of this book varied with every case. Two children (Cases 20 and 24) had already seen psychiatrists in their respective children's hospitals before coming to school. Two others (Cases 47 and 35) had been referred to a child guidance clinic, one from an infant welfare clinic and the other from a clinic for spastic children before reaching school age.

In general, however, the existence of emotional disturbances or behaviour problems became apparent in the ordinary course of school life; when taking the history from the mother at a routine medical inspection, from the observations of the teaching staff, or from the reports of the caseworkers. Such children were then carefully observed, and there were informal exchanges of opinion between the headmistress, the school doctor and Sister, caseworkers, and frequently the class teacher. If necessary, the parent would be invited for a more detailed discussion of the child's difficulties.

The school environment, and the skilful handling of the children's problems by the staff, usually resulted in improvements in the children's reactions to their problems. In some, however, it became clear that a child's particular difficulties were too deep-seated and too closely associated with the home environment to respond without more intensive help. This help was freely available from the trained caseworkers of the Invalid Children's Aid Association, working for the School Care Committee. The regular home-visiting, weekly or fortnightly, not only threw light on the nature of the problems involved, but helped to prepare the parents to accept recommendations for child guidance or other psychiatric help where this was considered necessary.

TABLE 15
Referrals, recommendations, outcome, remarks re C.G.C.

Case No.	Referred by	Regular treatment	Recommendation from Psychiatrist		Parents	Remarks
			Hosp. Supervision	CGC Supervision		
2	SMO (directly) mother's request	Yes (CGC)			Yes	For attendance after operation
5	SMO (PCC)			Yes	Yes	Supervision considered sufficient. (Marked speech defect)
13	SMO (PCC) (Educ. psychol.)			Yes	Yes	Continued to receive supervision caseworker
20	DMO (directly) mother's request	Yes (hospital)			Yes	Regular supervision psychiatric dept. children's hospital
21	SMO (directly)	Yes (PSW)			Yes	Parents unable accept CGC but accept weekly home visits PSW
24	Consult. Physician (hospital)		Yes		Yes	Occasional supervision psychiatric dept children's hosp.
31	SMO (PCC)	Yes (hospital)	Yes (eventually)		Yes (initially)	Parents unable accept CGC
35	Consult. Physician (directly) spastics centre			Yes	Yes	Supervision considered sufficient. (Marked speech defect)
41	Consult. Physician (directly) (hospital)		Yes		Yes	Occasional supervision psych. dept. children's hospital
42	SMO (PCC)	Yes (CGC)			Yes (initially)	Parents unable accept CGC
47	AMO (directly) M & CW clinic	Yes (CGC)			Yes	Regular treatment accepted CGC
49	Consult. Physician (directly) (hospital)	Yes (Educ. psychol.)			Yes	Parents unable accept CGC but accepted weekly visit to Educ. psychol. at CGC

Educ. psychol.—educational psychologist
PSW—psychiatric social worker
CGC—child guidance clinic

PCC—Problem Cases Conference
AMO—Assistant Medical Officer
M & CW—Maternity and Child Welfare

CHILDREN REFERRED FOR CHILD GUIDANCE

Twelve children were referred either to a hospital psychiatric department or to a local child guidance clinic. Details of these referrals are given in Table 11, Chapter 6.

Four of these children were referred to the Problem Cases Conference by the school doctor. This is the procedure normally followed, except where the referrals are from one hospital department to another, or in exceptional circumstances, or before the child reaches school age.

The procedure for the referral of schoolchildren for child guidance in London is the same both for handicapped children and for children in an ordinary school. Any child in the London County Council area with behaviour problems can be referred by the school doctor, or the headmistress, or occasionally by the School Care Committee in association with the headmistress, to a Problem Cases Conference. Only in cases of emergency, or exceptional circumstances, does the school doctor refer the child directly to a psychiatrist with, of course, the agreement of the head and of one or both parents. The referrals normally follow detailed discussions at a school medical inspection. The full discussion with the people mainly concerned before a child is referred aims to secure the maximum cooperation, especially from the parents.

The Problem Cases Conference, with representatives from the divisional medical office, the educational officer, the school care organizer, and other social agencies who have been involved with the family, considers every aspect of the case, including facilities for treatment, before referral for psychiatric treatment.

Three of the four children concerned were recommended by the Problem Cases Conference for child guidance, and the fourth (Case 13) for continued casework. (See p. 132.)

These cases will be described in some detail since they illustrate some of the psychological problems of handicapped children, and some of the predisposing causes of their maladjustment. They also throw some light on the difficulties of persuading parents to accept the need for child guidance.

In the first case (Case 42, a child with severe haemophilia), where regular treatment was recommended but failed to materialize, the psychiatrist at the local child guidance clinic reported 'a chronic anxiety state of a fairly severe degree' in the child. He also described the mother as 'depressed and defeated ... her anxiety and guilt excessive ... in great need of support'. A note was added that 'the prognosis must be uncertain in view of the father's possible hostility'. Considerable improvement, both at school and at home, followed the diagnostic interview, the occasional visits to the clinic and periodic home visits by the psychiatric social worker.

The mother also received considerable help and support from her attendance and discussions with the doctor at the birth control clinic. She was able, after some time and much discussion, to take a new and more interesting job serving in a shop, with more responsibility and contact with people. Later the family was rehoused in an attractive small house with garden, and both the family situation and the child's mental and physical health greatly improved.

In the second case (31), a child with an atrial septal defect and scoliosis, the psychiatrist found the child 'very depressed and full of resentment', and advised regular interviews with a view to psychotherapy. 'Although the mother's hostility, at least during this interview . . . was not really so extreme as might have been expected from the reports', she was unable to accept regular treatment, but was encouraged to return at any time. Although this child also showed some improvement, following the diagnostic interview and firm and sympathetic handling at school, the improvement has not been maintained in secondary school, nor has the mother yet been able to accept regular treatment.

In the third case (21), the child with spastic quadriplegia and mental retardation, arrangements were made at the diagnostic interview for the psychiatric social worker (from the Invalid Children's Aid Association) to continue home visits. The visits were carried out weekly over a period of eighteen months, and the parents were helped to understand and accept the child's limitations.

In the fourth case (5), the child with athetoid paraplegia and marked speech defect, the psychiatrist considered that the child's difficulties in settling into a new school were now resolved, and that he should be seen again only if further problems arose.

The fifth case (13), a child with a spinal tumour treated by radium, had been referred for child guidance with the agreement of the educational psychologist attached to the school, and the hospital at which she was treated. In addition to her severe current illness, Sally was anxious, timid and withdrawn as a result of extreme marital disharmony, a long period 'in care', a father suffering from chronic alcoholism, and a mother who had previously been admitted to a mental hospital. The Problem

Cases Conference in this instance decided to recommend the continuation of the regular casework which had been undertaken weekly by the Invalid Children's Aid Association. It was essential to keep the child under supervision, but the mother was considered too disturbed to accept or benefit from attendance at a child guidance clinic, and the child would not have been allowed or able to go without her.

Two cases were referred, at the mother's request, by the Divisional Medical Officer and the School Medical Officer respectively. The former (Case 20) 'in spite of five years of chronic osteomyelitis and all that has been involved in this . . . has remained emotionally healthy and un-damaged to a surprising extent', and is seen periodically. The latter (Case 2) is awaiting regular treatment at a child guidance clinic pending further operative treatment for his hemiplegia.

The eighth child (Case 47), who suffered from muscular dystrophy, had been attending a child guidance clinic regularly for three years. Initially referred for severe temper tantrums, he was then found to have muscular dystrophy. His many emotional difficulties included a tense and perfectionist mother, and a robust and athletic father (a firm believer in chastisement) who found it difficult to adjust his disciplinary methods to this child's and his younger brother's handicap.

The ninth case (41), a child with Fallot's tetralogy, was referred for enuresis and encopresis to their psychiatric department by the consultant pediatrician at the hospital after considerable discussion and correspond-ence with the school. In this case the mother was exceedingly anxious and was receiving support through weekly visits by the school caseworker from the Invalid Children's Aid Association. The home visits continue, and in addition the child is seen occasionally in the psychiatric depart-ment of the hospital.

The tenth case is of particular interest from the point of view of the school. This child (Case 24) was under the supervision of the psychiatric department of the hospital for severe tantrums and behaviour disorders, was severely retarded, and was being considered for a possible hemi-spherectomy. Nevertheless, after about eighteen months in school she had improved so much that only occasional appointments in the psychi-atric department were considered necessary.

The eleventh child (Case 49) was referred by the hospital consultant pediatrician for remedial teaching at a child guidance clinic. The urgent need for child guidance had long been recognized by the hospital staff, the school, the caseworker *and* the mother, but this was ultimately the only way in which she was able to accept help. The child suffered from severe haemophilia, and at eight years of age literally 'wrapped himself up in his own baby shawl each night to go to sleep'. At times he was spoon fed by his mother 'to get anything down him'. She also perceived that 'he uses his disability to get his own way.'

The twelfth case (35), a child with athetoid spastic paraplegia and severe speech defect, was referred from a spastic centre before coming to the school for severe and constant temper tantrums, and advice about residential placement. She was found to be highly intelligent and frustrated. Following discussion, residential placement was no longer acceptable to the mother nor was Eveline accepted for regular child guidance. She has subsequently shown considerable improvement in school. Regular speech therapy enabled her to overcome some of the frustrations due to lack of communication, and her temper tantrums are accordingly less frequent and severe. The mother is also receiving support from regular visits by the caseworker, and although she has great difficulty in adjusting herself to this severely handicapped child, some improvement has been made in their relationship.

To Summarize the Cases Referred for Child Guidance:

Twelve children had been referred.

Seven (Cases 31, 42, 20, 47, 21, 49, 2) had been accepted for regular treatment and of these, two (Cases 42 and 31) were able to tolerate occasional supervision only.

Two (Cases 41 and 24) had been accepted for hospital supervision.

One (Case 13) remained under supervision of the trained caseworker from the Invalid Children's Aid Association in view of the difficulties in securing sufficient cooperation from a psychotic mother to make regular child guidance possible.

Two (Cases 5 and 35) other children remained under similar supervision which was considered sufficient.

SUPERVISION BY CASEWORKERS

Supervision through home visiting by trained, full-time caseworkers (members of the Invalid Children's Aid Association working for the School Care Committee in a voluntary capacity) was carried out in all fifty cases. The number and frequency of the visits depended on the nature of the case, and the visits were organized by the caseworkers themselves, under the supervision of a consultant psychiatric social worker.

Verbal reports on the children were given at school medical inspections by the caseworkers, when present, and written reports were available at any time on request. These reports, covering different aspects of the case through contacts with hospital almoners, social workers and other social agencies, were of great value in the recurring discussions of problems facing the handicapped child and his family.

In the cases requiring intensive casework, parents were visited frequently to help them understand how the child's handicap affects family relationships, and how it may lead to emotional as well as practical difficulties. Parents were encouraged to accept the fact that in such circumstances ambivalent feelings toward the child are perfectly natural. They were helped to express freely their doubts and difficulties, their sense of guilt and failure, and their feelings of rejection. Where it became clear that the difficulties were too deep-seated for casework, decisions for psychiatric referral were taken only after the fullest discussion with the headmistress, the school doctor, the school Sister, the class teacher, the School Care Committee secretary and the parents.

Invaluable help continued to be given by the caseworkers concerned, in following up decisions for referral. They discussed the parents' doubts and difficulties about this at home, and gave them understanding support until treatment was available. Unfortunately, long intervals often occurred before a diagnostic interview could be arranged, and even longer (up to several months) before treatment could be started. When treatment was begun, the child guidance clinic normally kept in close touch with the caseworker and received further help in case of missed appointments, special visiting or liaison with the school. Intensive casework was, perhaps, most needed during the period in which referral was under consideration or pending treatment.

SCHOOL CONFERENCES

These were held in the normal course of school medical inspections as the need arose, and as described above. After discussion, decisions were reached relating to referrals for psychiatric advice, continuing casework, arrangements for recuperative holidays, making additional representations for rehousing, or whatever else was considered necessary.

Where the problem was primarily one of behaviour in school, lunch-hour discussions with the headmistress and her staff were arranged. The educational psychologist attached to the local child guidance clinic gave advice and guidance. With her cooperation, and with the full agreement of the headmistress and staff, arrangements were also made for monthly conferences, to include the psychiatrist or other members of the local child guidance clinic when necessary.

Owing to administrative difficulties these conferences were not fully established. If, however, such regular conferences could be achieved, they would undoubtedly benefit not only the children discussed, but would help to raise the level of understanding of handicapped children and their problems throughout the school and by all concerned.

Discussion

THIS survey was carried out to study the special problems of handicapped children and their families from the viewpoint of a school medical officer, and to illustrate these with cases from a primary day school for the physically handicapped.

It was intended to further understanding of the nature and extent of their problems, and to put forward ideas which might be of help in dealing with them.

Although the sample of fifty children from one day school for the physically handicapped is a small one, the general problems of these children relate to quite a significant section of the population. Kershaw states that 'Though perhaps fewer than 3 per cent of the population of a country may be actually handicapped, 10 or 15 per cent may have their lives complicated by their own disability or that of others.'

These figures refer only to physically handicapped children, but the problems of a family with a mentally handicapped child are, in many ways, very similar and the numbers involved greater. (Tizard and Grad, 1961).

The facts and figures given in this survey leave little doubt that 'A physical handicap, of itself, constitutes an emotional hazard and sooner or later will become an emotional challenge both for the child and his family.' Caplan, in *An Approach to Community Mental Health*, refers to the problems of a health department dealing with a thousand new cases a year of children with disabling physical handicaps—'all of whom have some form of emotional complications, and many of whom have explicit psychiatric symptomalogy.'

With this approach in mind, a particular attempt was made to study the type and extent of emotional problems as they affected the children, their siblings and parents.

The case material and the estimation of the numbers of children or parents showing varying degrees of emotional complications confirm the

Handicap

fact that the handicap is indeed an emotional hazard for both the children and their families. Furthermore, the case material confirms Dr. Caplan's opinion that 'a baby with a congenital abnormality creates a situation which requires immediate and specialized attention, particularly during the critical period of the first two months after birth.'

CONTINUITY OF SUPERVISION

The first weeks after the diagnosis of a congenital abnormality or severe handicap are undoubtedly a critical period. There are, however, many other critical periods during the child's development when advice and guidance are needed to prevent 'avoidable unhappiness and personality distortions for family and child.' (Caplan.)

For this reason it seems appropriate to recommend that every mother of a handicapped child should be seen by a psychiatric social worker, or almoner with a particular interest in this field, immediately a congenital abnormality or severe handicap is diagnosed, and before leaving hospital. Arrangements should be made for continued supervision in the home by caseworkers with a specialized training in this field, working in association with the family doctor, the Health Visitor, the hospital authorities, and later the educational psychologist and the school authorities. These specially trained caseworkers should be under the supervision of a consultant psychiatric social worker, and should be able to accept responsibility for handling the mental health problems that might arise. Hence there must be opportunities for in-service training and consultation. In London and the Home Counties the caseworkers of the Invalid Children's Aid Association generally meet these requirements. Their handling of casework and case discussions at school examinations have proved invaluable. Their previous knowledge of many of the children and their insight into family relationships has made possible the kind of team work which is in the best interests of the children.

There follows, therefore, the recommendation for regular case conferences in school to which the educational psychologist or members of the child guidance unit could be invited. This arrangement, in addition to the opportunity it provides for referring cases for full investigation and treatment, is in close agreement with the proposals made by Caplan.

Discussion

FACTORS ADVERSELY AFFECTING EMOTIONAL ADJUSTMENT TO THE
HANDICAP BY THE CHILD AND THE PARENTS

An attempt was also made to study the factors adversely affecting the emotional adjustment of the child to his handicap and of the parents to their child's handicap.

The main factors affecting the child's adjustment appeared to be the severity of the handicap; the degree and quality of parental anxiety, particularly the extent of rejection; and the presence of marital friction or a broken home. Factors relating to the parents themselves appeared to be their fears about the child's future; his prospects of work and family life; the ultimate prospect of institutional care; anxieties about future pregnancies; problems of birth control; marital disharmonies and separations; parental ill health, physical or mental, and the effects of social conditions.

It was difficult to estimate the relative importance of these different factors, and still more difficult to estimate the factors which influenced the parents' ability to make a satisfactory adjustment, except in the most general terms. A realistic acceptance of the handicap, by both parents, and parental harmony appeared to be the over-riding factors for the success of the child's adjustment.

The key importance of these factors is perhaps best illustrated by quoting the cases of two children, both severe cases of athetoid cerebral palsy with severe speech defects, whose parents had been told in the first few weeks of their child's life that the child would probably be blind, deaf and an imbecile. In the first case, although he was of above-average intelligence, the child also had severe loss of hearing. The adjustment of mother and child, however, appeared excellent. The mother accepted his handicap calmly and realistically and the child appeared happy and well adjusted. He made good progress in social maturity as well as in his education in spite of all his difficulties.

In the second case, with an equally intelligent but severely handicapped child (though without any loss of hearing), the mother had obvious difficulties in accepting the handicap—she openly expressed her disappointment and envy of other women with large and healthy families. She accepted work which took her out of the house an hour after the child returned from school each day, and left the care of the child largely to the grandmother. There was considerable disharmony in the home, especially between the grandmother and son-in-law. The child was quite unable to accept her handicap, and suffered from marked frustration. She developed severe temper tantrums, and was left to scream in her room until exhausted, since her mother could find no other way of coping with her during her tantrums.

This mother received little guidance in the handling of her daughter until the child was admitted to school. Then gradually over a period of two years, with weekly visits from the caseworker, there was an improvement in the child and in her relationship with her mother. Unhappy marital relations, differing attitudes, and lack of emotional support and guidance in the early crucial years appear to have been factors in this failure to make a satisfactory adjustment.

PROBLEMS OF MEDICAL SUPERVISION: THE ROLE OF THE SCHOOL MEDICAL OFFICER

There were considerable gaps in the overall continuous supervision of the handicapped child, since it was possible to carry out only one routine medical examination a year at school.

It was clear from 98 per cent of the cases that once the child was referred to hospital for his handicap, the general practitioner considered the hospital fully responsible and took no further part in the supervision of the handicap or the related problems.

In some cases, hospital supervision, even of the handicap, lacked continuity. It would appear that, with a few exceptions, satisfactory supervision of the child requires more than six-monthly visits to a special clinic or hospital out-patient department.

The potential role of the school doctor, therefore, is one of considerable responsibility. He or she should be in fairly constant touch with the hospital, in relation to treatment (physiotherapy, etc.), appliances (repair and renewal) and general progress. Reports should be exchanged regarding the child's progress and difficulties at school. These may assist the consultant in his assessment, particularly in cases of epilepsy or severe behaviour disorders. Contact with the general practitioner, particularly in the case of intercurrent illness or sedative therapy, is also important. The single most important task of the school doctor appears to be to co-ordinate the approach of all the agencies dealing with the child. A secondary related task includes convening case conferences at school to consider the problems of particular children as the need arises.

This work involves a detailed knowledge of the child and his environ-

---

ment, and requires more time and more frequent routine examinations of each child. It also underscores the need for the proposed regular case conferences at school.

It is of interest to note in relation to some of the problems of early diagnosis (particularly in the case of cerebral palsies) that had the 'at risk' registers now in use in the maternity and child welfare clinics been available and used correctly when the children in the survey were infants, 50 per cent of them would have been included as requiring close supervision. When the nineteen acquired handicaps are excluded the figures are even more striking, for 75 per cent of the congenital or neo-natal handicaps, had they attended a clinic operating an 'at risk' register, would have been specifically followed up at frequent intervals. Of the 10 per cent who were Rhesus-negative, it is probable that with the knowledge now available, the ensuing handicaps might have been less severe, or even prevented altogether.

SOCIAL PROBLEMS

An attempt was made to determine the main social problems of families with handicapped children. The outstanding need appeared to be that of suitable housing accommodation; a ground-floor flat or a house with a garden.

This could transform the situation. Even if the child were chairborne, or only able to sit on the grass, there would at least be a place to play in safety and grow things. Yet the great majority of these children lived in poor, overcrowded homes, or high up in large blocks of flats, where it was difficult to get them up and down stairs, and often impossible to let them play in the fresh air without a special excursion.

Provision of a special housing priority category is therefore recommended, to provide suitable accommodation for all severely handicapped children and their families.

EDUCATIONAL PROBLEMS

There was little doubt of the parents' appreciation of the benefits of a day school for the physically handicapped. The benefits were equally obvious in the case of those children who knew no other, and those who had been transferred from ordinary school. The latter were able to relax and make friends more easily because they were no longer the 'odd man out', and consequently made to feel inferior. The handicapped children obviously responded to the atmosphere of friendly acceptance.

Although the present tendency is to keep as many handicapped children as possible in normal schools, and to return them to ordinary schools as soon as possible, it appears that there will always be a minority who need the sheltered atmosphere, the physical therapy, the care and supervision, and the understanding of their special problems, which can be found in the special schools for the physically handicapped.

CHAPTER 12

Summary and Recommendations

THE SURVEY

A SURVEY of fifty physically handicapped children and their families from a primary day school for physically handicapped children in London is described.

Thirty-one of the fifty children had congenital or neo-natal handicaps, including fourteen children with cerebral palsy. Nineteen children had acquired handicaps, including eight with poliomyelitis, and seven with conditions leading to a secondary cerebral palsy.

PROBLEMS OF MEDICAL SUPERVISION

The pattern of medical supervision was similar in 98 per cent of the cases. It consisted of periodic (usually six-monthly) visits to hospital, and an annual medical inspection by the school doctor. In addition, children with cardiac, orthopaedic or cerebral palsy conditions were seen once or twice a year by the Council's visiting consultants. In only one case was a child under the supervision of his own general practitioner on account of his handicap; in every other case the children were seen by their general practitioners only for unrelated illness.

The number of admissions to hospital varied from nought to thirty, the average number per child was five and a half. The duration of the admissions ranged from one night to four years. The average length of time spent in hospital for the forty-nine children admitted was thirty-two weeks.

Ninety-four per cent of the mothers thought that the doctor should tell the parents 'as soon as he suspects physical or mental defects'.

Sixty-four per cent of the mothers indicated satisfaction with the way in which they had been told and fourteen per cent were critical. Twenty-two per cent complained of delay, either in confirming the handicap or in being told about it.

Handicap

Fifty-eight per cent of the mothers stated that when they were first told of their child's handicap, they were *not* able to discuss with the doctor what the diagnosis meant, what the child would be like, or where they could go for advice.

Fifty-two per cent of the mothers expressed a need for more specialist advice about their handicapped child. Sixteen per cent of the mothers spontaneously expressed a wish for occasional interviews with the specialist to discuss the handling of the child and his problems.

PSYCHOLOGICAL PROBLEMS

The Referral Rate for Child Guidance

In the fifty cases studied, the referral rate was 24 per cent, three times higher than the average rate for ordinary schools as estimated from three pilot surveys recorded in the Underwood Report (Ministry of Education, 1955).

The Prevalence of Emotional Problems

According to the scoring standards used, fifty-two per cent of the children showed moderately severe or severe emotional difficulties.

Thirty-one per cent of the parents showed moderately severe or severe degrees of rejection of the handicapped child.

(In 18 per cent, one or both parents deserted either permanently or temporarily.)

Fifty-six per cent of the parents showed moderately severe or severe degrees of over-anxiety and over-protection.

Twenty-one per cent of the siblings showed signs of considerable emotional difficulties in adjusting to the handicap.

Factors Affecting the Child's Adjustment to the Handicap

The severity of the handicap, the prognosis, the degree and quality of parental anxiety (with special reference to rejection) and the nature of family relationships, including the effect of poor marital relations or a broken home, have been shown to affect the child's adjustment.

Factors Adversely Affecting the Parents' Emotional Adjustment to the Handicap

Eighty per cent of the parents acknowledged that anxiety about the child's future constituted a considerable worry for them.

Eighty per cent of the cases of severe or cogenital handicaps expressed their fears of future pregnancies.

Considerable anxiety as to the cause of the handicap appeared to be present in 84 per cent of the cases, i.e. in all but the eight cases which were acquired handicaps.

SOCIAL PROBLEMS

Sixty-four per cent of the mothers experienced difficulties in attending hospital for supervision, treatment or visiting, because of the time involved, travelling, the cost of fares, the care of siblings or ill health.

Problems of unsuitable or overcrowded housing accommodation appeared to add to the difficulties of the great majority of the families and in 88 per cent of the families a ground-floor flat and garden were the first special consideration requested of the Local Authorities.

Forty-two per cent of the parents reported their leisure activities severely restricted by the handicapped child.

Fifty per cent of the parents found holidays complicated and restricted by the handicapped child.

Supervision by means of home-visiting and casework was carried out by members of the Invalid Children's Aid Association attached to the School Care Committee, in 88 per cent of the families and by a number of other agencies, on occasion. Twelve per cent had not been visited prior to the survey. These visits were welcomed by 68 per cent of the mothers, tolerated by 16 per cent and resented by 4 per cent.

Thirty-six per cent of the parents belonged to a parents' association for the particular handicap, and a further 20 per cent asked to be put in touch with one during the interviews.

The number of mothers suffering from chronic illness or physical disability in the fifty cases was thirty-eight. In addition, almost two-thirds of the mothers suffered from varying degrees of anxiety, depression, tension and fatigue, which appeared directly related to the handicapped child.

EDUCATIONAL PROBLEMS

The loss of school time due to hospital admissions has been given for each child. The average number of admissions was five and a half and the average duration was thirty-two weeks.

The amount of school time lost for therapy (physio, speech and occupational) for fifteen children varied from fifteen minutes for one child to five hours for another. The average loss was one hour and thirty-four minutes a week.

The percentage attendance at school was 81·7. This figure of about 20 per cent absenteeism is about twice the normal rate for children in ordinary schools.

Twenty-four per cent of the children suffered from speech defects (impaired communication). Forty-two per cent had impaired muscular coordination. The loss of development-stimulating experiences and the effects of emotional retardation were also studied.

A graded assessment of each pupil's 'ability to deal with the problems presented by day-to-day living in view of his physical, or physical and mental, handicap' was made.

Twelve per cent showed much below average ability.

Thirty-two per cent showed below average ability.

Thirty-eight per cent showed average ability.

Eighteen per cent showed above average ability.

The effects of school life on the handicapped child were discussed and illustrated by examples.

The parents' opinions of the physically handicapped school were sought in relation to its advantages and disadvantages compared with ordinary schools.

Sixty-eight per cent of the parents thought there were no disadvantages.

Thirty-two per cent thought there were, or might be, disadvantages, chiefly from an educational standpoint.

(Every parent referred to one or more advantages; 38 per cent to the care and supervision given the children, 24 per cent to the school transport, etc.)

RECOMMENDATIONS

Much closer overall supervision of the handicapped child and his family, at every stage and in relation to all his problems: physical, psychological, social and educational.

Pre-school

Every mother of a handicapped child should be seen by a psychiatric social worker, or an almoner with a particular interest in this field, when a congenital abnormality or severe handicap is diagnosed, and before leaving hospital. Arrangements should be made for continued supervision in the home by caseworkers with special training in this field, working in association with the family doctor, the health visitor, the hospital authorities, and later, the educational psychologist and the school authorities.

School

During the child's school career, the need for closer overall supervision can perhaps best be met by the school doctor, in close cooperation with the hospitals, the visiting consultants, the family doctor, the caseworker visiting the family, the educational psychologist and the staff of the school. This would involve a more detailed knowledge of each child and his problems, and more frequent medical examinations.

There should be a specially trained full-time caseworker attached to each school for the physically handicapped (in preference the specialized caseworker already visiting the majority of handicapped children in the area, and in contact with other caseworkers for physically handicapped children in the catchment area of the school). She should attend every medical examination, arrange for visits to every home as necessary, and work in close cooperation with the medical and teaching staff.

OTHER PROPOSALS FOR CONSIDERATION

The need for a special housing category, to provide suitable ground-floor accommodation, with a garden, for handicapped children and their families.

A scheme for trained 'sitters-in', possibly by means of a voluntary rota from the Red Cross, St John Ambulance Brigade, the various societies and associations for handicapped children, retired teachers or nurses, etc., to allow the parents of handicapped children to go out together, perhaps once a month.

A play centre for handicapped children, with transport provided perhaps two or three times a week during the school holidays, to relieve the strain on families living in overcrowded or unsuitable housing conditions.

Handicap

A handicapped children's voluntary car service, to take children for their appointments, and to provide an escort when necessary (as in parental ill health), without throwing additional burdens on the ambulance service, or subjecting the children to the long periods of waiting often involved.

REFERENCES

APLEY, J. and MACKEITH, R. (1962). *The Child and his Symptoms: A Psychosomatic Approach.* Oxford: Blackwell Scientific Publications.

BOWLBY, J. (1951). *Maternal Care and Mental Health.* Geneva: World Health Organization (Monograph Series, No. 2).

CAPLAN, G. (1961). *An Approach to Community Mental Health.* London: Tavistock Publications; New York: Grune & Stratton.

KERSHAW, J. D. (1961). *Handicapped Children.* London: Heinemann Medical Books.

MINISTRY OF EDUCATION (1955). *Report of the Committee on Maladjusted Children* (Underwood Committee). London: H.M.S.O.

ROBERTSON, J. (1958). *Young Children in Hospital.* London: Tavistock Publications.

TIZARD, J. and GRAD, J. C. (1961). *The Mentally Handicapped and their Families.* London: Oxford University Press.

APPENDICES

APPENDIX I

Questionnaire on the Problems of Handicapped Children and their Families (NA=not applicable: DK= don't know).

1. Diagnosis   Cerebral Palsy   1
   Poliomyelitis   2
   Congenital heart   3
   Haemophilia   4
   Other congenital defects   5
   Other   6

2. Short History

3. Extent of handicap   Slight   1
   Moderate   2
   Severe   3

4. Other handicaps   Hearing   1
   Visual   2
   Epileptic   3
   Maladjusted   4
   Speech   5
   None   6
   Backward   7

5. Is he paralysed in any way?   NA   0
   DK   1
   Note extent of disability.

6. If paralysed
   (a) Has there been any difficulty in obtaining   NA   0
   treatment or advice?   DK   1
   (b) Has he received special education or training,   NA   0
   other than at a PH school, because of this?   DK   1

7. Is his eyesight affected?　o
　　　　　　　　　　　　　　I

   Has there been any difficulty in obtaining　o
   advice or treatment?　　　　　　　　　　I

8. Is his hearing affected?　　　　　　　　　o
　　　　　　　　　　　　　　　　　　　　　I

   Has there been any difficulty in obtaining　o
   advice or treatment?　　　　　　　　　　I

9. Does he have any speech defects?　　o
　　　　　　　　　　　　　　　　　　I
　　　　　　　　　Cleft palate　　　2
　　　　　　　　　Stammering　　　3
　　　　　　　　　Slurred speech　　4
　　　　　　　　　Other (describe)　5

   Has there been any difficulty in obtaining　o
   advice or treatment?　　　　　　　　　　I

10. Have there been any special dental problems?　o
　　　　　　　　　　　　　　　　　　　　　　　I

   Has there been any difficulty in obtaining　o
   advice or treatment?　　　　　　　　　　I

11. Does he have fits or turns?　　o
　　　　　　　　　　　　　　　　I
　　If yes, (a) when did he have his last fit?
　　　　　　(b) how often do they occur?
　　　　　　　　at least once a day　　2
　　　　　　　　,, ,, ,, ,, week　　3
　　　　　　　　,, ,, ,, ,, month　　4
　　　　　　　　less frequently　　5
　　　　　　(c) are these momentary blank spells　　GM　2
　　　　　　　　(or blackouts) or does he fall　　PM　3
　　　　　　　　down or have convulsions?　　Both　4
　　　　　　(d) do they occur　by day　2
　　　　　　　　　　　　　　by night　3
　　　　　　　　　　　　　　both　　4

Has there been any difficulty in obtaining   o
advice or treatment?   1

12. Does he have persistent colds or coughs or chest trouble?   o
                                                                1

Has there been any difficulty in obtaining   o
advice or treatment?   1

13. Are there any other health problems?   o
                                           1

14. Has he ever attended a Child Guidance Clinic? o
                                                  1

15. General health is poor   2
                 fair   3
                 good   4
                 a severe problem   5
                 stable health with severe
                 physical incapacity   6

16. Supervision and treatment
    He is seen at regular intervals by the GP   o
                              hospital OP   1
                              hospital special 2
                              clinic
                                    SMO   3
    seen by the GP only when special illness   4

17. Treatment (describe)

18. He has physiotherapy at a special hospital clinic   o
                          general   ,,   ,,   1
                          school clinic   2
                          privately   3
                          none   4

19. He has speech therapy at a special hospital clinic   0
                                general   1
                                school clinic   2
                                privately   3
                                none   4

20. How many hours a week does he have treatment? _____

How many hours school work does he have to miss a week? _____

Appliances

21. Does he wear any appliances   0
                     glasses   1
                     hearing aid   2
                     special boots or shoes   3
                     none   4

22. Who supervises his appliances (describe)
How often?

23. Who repairs or renews appliances (describe)
How often?

24. Are there any difficulties on obtaining, repairing   0
or renewing appliances?   1

25. Has he ever been admitted to hospital or convalescent home?   0
                                                              1

26. How often?   hospital————times
                    convalescent home (without
                          prior admission to hospital)————times

27. For how long each time (weeks)
                                     Total _____

28. At what age(s)

29. Was visiting in hospital allowed, and possible?   0   NA
                                                       1   DK
            If yes, visits daily   2
                     twice weekly or   3
                     more weekly   4
                     once or twice a month   5
                     less frequently   6

30. What were child's reactions to visits?
    (describe: upset, apparently indifferent, etc.)

31. Has there been any difficulty in attending for supervision, treatment
    or visiting?
                              None   0
            Yes, owing to: the time factor   1
                            travelling   2
                            care of siblings   3
                            cost   4
                            parental ill-health 5
                            other reasons (specify) 6

PART II—EDUCATIONAL DEVELOPMENT

32. Other previous tuition under the Education Acts
                          None   0
                          Ordinary day school   1
                          Home tuition (L.C.C.) 2
                          ,,   ,, (private) 3
                          Hospital tuition   4
                          Other   5

33. I.Q. (where already available through educational psychologist)

34. Progress in Reading   —   Scale
              Arithmetic   —   Scale

35. School Report—Teachers' Questionnaire (National Survey)
    (Appendix A)

PART III—PROBLEMS OF MANAGEMENT

36. Is he incontinent?   0
                                                           1
    (a) urine only by day and night 2
               by night 3
    Urine, faeces by day and night 4
               by night 5
    (b) napkins are not needed 6
               washed at home 7
               laundry 8

37. How often does mother take him out with her?
    daily 1
    2–3 times a week 2
    once a week 3
    occasionally 4
    rarely 5

38. If mother rarely takes him out is this because of
    Problems of management 1 NA
    She is embarrassed 2 DK

39. Is he ever left alone for more than a few minutes?
    Not at all 0
    in a room 1
    in the house 2

40. Is anyone prevented from going out to work because of him?
    No 0
    Yes, mother 1
    Someone else (specify)
    —————— 2
    Part-time 3
    Full-time 4

157

41. Does anyone, besides mother, look after him when he is at home?

Father	1	NA	
Siblings	2	DK	
Relations	3		
Others	4		

42. How often does mother leave him to someone else's care?

Never	0	NA	
Emergency	1	DK	
Occasionally	2		
Frequently	3		

43. What does father do as his share of caring for the child when the child is at home?

Nothing	0	NA	
Occasionally helps	1	DK	
Helps mother with household duties	2		
Looks after him when mother is out	3		
Takes him and spends time with him when free	4		
Shares completely in minding and occupying him	5		

44. If father takes *no* part in caring for the child is this because

He does not want to do so	2	NA	
Mother will not let him	3	DK	
He has never looked after the others	4		
Other reasons	5		

45. Are parents' leisure activities — Not restricted 0 NA

[*Note*—Any different from what they would be if child were normal]   They include him but he is a 'tie' 1 DK

Severely restricted because of the child 2

46. How often does mother go out, for pleasure, without the child?
(e.g. friends, cinema, club, church)

No mother	0	
At least once a week	1	NA
At least once a month	2	DK
Less often	3	

47. How often does father go out, for pleasure, without the child?
(e.g. friends, cinema, pub, football, club)

No father	0	NA
At least once a week	1	DK
At least once a month	2	
Less often	3	

48. Are the family's holiday arrangements complicated in any way by the child?

NA 0
DK 1
No holidays anyhow————X
If yes, describe how
Prompt:

Not possible to find accommodation with him	2
It makes holiday accommodation difficult to find	3
Financial difficulties	4
Parents cannot go together	5
Other—describe	6

49. Does the child go on holiday?

Not at all	0
With parents	1
With institution	2
With school	3
With others	4

50. Has he been in any serious trouble during the past year, at home or in school? (describe)

0
1
DK

Appendix I

51. Have the neighbours complained about him?   NA   o
                                                                                DK   I

52. What do the parents think will happen to the child in the future if either or both die?

Institution	I
Relatives	2
Hope he will be able to look after himself	3
Don't think about it	4

53. Is the problem of what will happen to him in the future

no problem	o
a major worry	I
a cause of family conflict	2
a worry but solution has been accepted	3

The Household

54. Composition of the family   Child's position: of

Relationship to child	Died	Age	Marital status	Occupation or school

55. Composition of the Household

Relation to child	Sex	Age	Marital status	Occupation or school

56. Family Income

	N.A.B.	Head of household	Other earners	Housekeeping Allowance minus rent	As stated by
Nil					
0–£3 a week					
£3–£5					
£5–£7½					
£7½–£10					
£10–£20					
over £20					

Rent per week

57. Social class rating   Non-manual   1
                       Skilled   2
                       Semi-skilled   3
                       Unskilled   4

Housing

58. Type of dwelling   House   1
                      Flat   2
                      Rooms   3
                      Other   4

59. How many rooms are there? (exclude scullery and bathroom)   ____

60. Crowding index   No. of people

                  _____   _____

                   No. of rooms

61. Does the child share a bed when he is at home?   0   NA
                                                    1   DK
     If yes, with how many?   Siblings   2
                               Parents   3
                               Others   4

62. Does he share a room?   0   NA

                                  1   DK

        If yes, with how many   Siblings   2

                      ——Parents   3

                       Others   4

63. Is there a garden?   None   0   NA

                 Shared with others   1   DK

                 For own use   2

64. Is there a bathroom?   None   0   NA

                     Shared   1   DK

                     For own use   2

65. Is there a kitchen or scullery?   None   0   NA

                              Shared   1   DK

                              For own use   2

66. Is there an inside W.C.?   None   0   NA

                         Shared   1   DK

                         For own use   2

67. Is there an outside W.C.?   None   0   NA

                         Shared   1   DK

                         For own use   2

68. Are there structural faults which make the house uncomfortable to live in?

                                           NA   0

                                           DK   1

                     Damp   2

                     Draughty   3

                     Leaks   4

                     Poor drainage   5

                     Other   6

69. Other notes on housing—

Family Health

70. Is any member of the family or household (state relationship to child)

in an institution	1
mentally backward	2
under treatment at psychiatric hospital	3
„ „ „ general „ or by a doctor	4
physically handicapped	5
epileptic	6
suffers from poor health generally	7
(describe)	

71. Is mother concerned about the health or behaviour of any other member of the family or household (state relationship to child)?

Anxious	1
Depressed	2
Delinquent	3
In poor health	4
(describe)	
Other	5

Mother's Health

72. Does mother suffer from any chronic illness or physical disability?

NA   0
DK   1

If yes, describe

73. Is mother very depressed?

Never	0	NA
Sometimes	1	DK
Frequently	2	
Always	3	

74. Does she sometimes feel that everything is too much for her and she cannot cope?

NA   0
DK   1

75. Does she worry so much that she cannot sleep? NA   0
                                                                'DK   1

76. Can she never relax but always has to be 'on the go'? NA   0
                                                                  DK   1

77. Does she complain of frequent headaches? NA   0
                                                                DK   1

78. Does she always feel tired and 'run-down'? NA   0
                                                                DK   1

79. Other notes about mother
      (Prompt—Menorrhagia, etc.)

PART IV—EMOTIONAL ADJUSTMENT

The Child

80. Breast feeding   Not at all   0
                            Under 3 months   1
                            Over 3 months   2

81. Feeding difficulties (describe)

82. Landmarks   At what age did he sit
                                                  walk
                                                  talk

83. Separations from mother (other than hospital, etc.)
      State duration in weeks
                            at age 0–17 mths.   1   weeks
                            18 mths.–4 yrs.   2   ,,
                            5–9 yrs.   3   ,,
      Describe—

      Prompting questions—Who looked after him?
                                              Any special circumstances?

84. Attitude to disability

   Is the child coping well with his handicap?   o

   Having considerable difficulties   1

   Unable to cope unaided   2

Describe—

Prompting questions—Does he try to hide his disability   1

   „   „   „   „ ignore „   „   2

   „   „   „   „ do both   3

   „   „   use his disability to
       get his own way?   4

Temperament and Conduct

85. Taking the child's behaviour and relationships with others as a whole, is he:—

	Not at all	Some-what	Very
Sensitive or highly strung	1	2	3
Shy or withdrawn	4	5	6
Aggressive	7	8	9
Other (state)	–	X	V
Teacher agrees	1		
disagrees	2		

86. Does he usually seem tired and sluggish or lively and energetic as compared to others?

   Almost completely apathetic   2

   Under-active   3

   As lively as most   4

   Livelier and more energetic   5

   Uncontrollably excitable   6

   DK

87. How often is he restless and fidgety (does he sit all day unless pushed to follow routine or is he usually walking around or restlessly moving some part of his body)?

Rarely or never	2
Occasionally—e.g. when he has, nothing to do	3
Frequently restless and fidgety but not always	4
Always on the go, never still	5
	DK

88. Is he nervous or timid (afraid of noises, of the dark, shy of strangers, afraid to venture out of the house alone)?

Extremely nervous even in a familiar environment	2
Rather nervous or timid	3
Not usually so	4
	DK

89. Does he stay by himself and avoid others or does he like being with people?

Solitary, ignores everyone	2
Friendly with others and likes company	3
Cannot bear to be left alone	4
	DK

90. Does he resist, refuse or fight against doing the ordinary things expected of him (such as dressing, washing, going to bed, getting up)?

Never	2
Once in a while	3
Fairly often	4
Almost always	5
	DK

91. How often does he fly into tempers or scream if he doesn't get his own way?

Rarely or never	2
Occasionally	3
About once a day	4
Constantly	5

92. Does he ever tease, pick on or bully others?

Never	2
Occasionally	3
Fairly often	4

93. Does he ever hit out or attack anyone?

Never	2
Occasionally	3
Fairly often (must be watched)	4

94. Does he tear up papers, magazines, clothing, or damage furniture, etc.?

Never	2
Occasionally	3
Fairly often (must be watched)	4

95. Is he very noisy?

Rarely	2
At times	3
Constantly	4

96. Is he a danger in the home, gas, fires, etc?

NA	0
DK	1

97. Has he any 'bad habits'?

(a) Comfort habits	Sucking	0
	Rocking	1
	Masturbating	2
	Other (specify)	3
(b) Tension habits	Picking	4
	Biting	5
	Tics	6
	Head banging	7
	Other (specify)	8
	Teacher agrees	X
	disagrees	V

167

Appendix I

98. Is his sleep disturbed?   NA   0
                              DK   1

99. Does he disturb others' sleep?   NA   0
                                     DK   1

100. Is he a loving, responsible and affectionate child?
                    Constantly demands attention   0
                    Like others   1
                    Does not seem to understand   2

The Parents

101. Are parents separated or divorced?   NA   0
                                          DK   1
        If yes—(a) legally or otherwise
               (b) when did they separate?
               (c) what was the reason?

102. Are there frequent quarrels between mother and father?
            (a) about the child   NA   0
                                        DK   1
            (b) about other matters   NA   0
                                        DK   1

103. How has the child affected the marriage relationship?
            Improved it   1   NA
            Had no effect   2   DK
            Made it worse   3
            Other   4
        Illustrate—

104. How did the knowledge that their child was handicapped affect
     the parents' attitude to having other children?
            They decided not to have any more   1
            They were worried about having others in case
            another handicapped child was born   2
            They worried about having others as it would be
            a burden to have a handicapped sibling   3
            Other   4
                                                                  NA
                                                                  DK

168

105. Did the parents agree in their attitude to having more children?

    No   0   NA

    Yes   1   DK

    Did not discuss it   2

106. Did they seek advice whether to have more children?   NA   0

                                                                            DK   1

    If yes (a) From whom (including friends, neighbours)

             (b) What advice was given

107. Does mother ever feel ashamed and embarrassed by people knowing about the child's handicap?   NA   0

                                     DK   1

    If yes—So much so that she avoids people   2

            So much so that she rarely takes him out   3

            She feels embarrassed but tries to overcome this   4

            She does not care what people think   5

108. Does father ever feel ashamed and embarrassed by people knowing about the child's handicap?   NA   0

                                     DK   1

    If yes—So much so that he avoids people   2

            So much so that he rarely takes him out   3

            He feels embarrassed but tries to overcome this   4

            He does not care what people think   5

109. Are the neighbours and relations unkind or critical of the child?

    Not at all   0   NA

    Somewhat   1   DK

    A great deal   2

110. Does mother feel that he is too much of a burden to be left at times with people whom she would ask to look after her normal child?

                                 NA   0

                                 DK   1

111. (a) What do the parents say are the most distressing things about having a handicapped child?

    (b) And what are the nicest things about him? (open question)

Appendix I

Group Participation

112. Are the parents members of a parents' association, if so, which

    (a) Mother   NA   0
                            DK   1
           attends meetings   2
           does not attend meetings   3
    (b) Father   NA   4   (No)
                            DK   5   (Yes)
           attends meetings   6
           does not attend meetings   7

113. Are the parents practising members of any religion or church?
    (a) Mother   NA   0
                            DK   1
           attends meetings   2
           does not attend meetings   3
    (b) Father   NA   0
                            DK   1
           attends meetings   2
           does not attend meetings   3
    State religion

114. How often do parents attend church services per month?
    Mother   times
    Father   times

115. Do parents belong to any clubs or societies?   NA   0
                                             DK   1
    If yes, give the name of the club, how often they attend
    meetings and any offices either have held

116. Have parents ever seriously tried to find out about any particular
    aspect of the child's handicap?
                          NA   0
                          DK   1

170

Prompt: Through Reading 2
              Attending lectures 3
              Discussing with other parents 4
              Other 5

117. Attitude to disability—Mother
     Is the mother able to cope with handicap   0
           having difficulty coping with the handicap   1
           unable to cope with handicap unaided   2
     Describe
     Prompting questions—
        Does she try to ignore his disability 3
         „ „ urge him to overcome it 4
         „ „ protect him from difficulties 5
         „ „ encourage his independence 6

118. Attitude to disability—Father—describe

The Siblings

119. Does the child's presence impede their work or play?   NA   0
                                                      DK   1

120. Does his presence interfere with their social
relationships? (e.g., neighbours won't play   NA   0
with them—unable to bring friends home)   DK   1

121. Does the child ill-treat siblings (e.g., baby)?   NA   0
                                                DK   1

122. Do they show marked jealousy or neurotic symptoms which can be
related to him?   NA   0
                DK   1

123. What is their attitude to him?
     Friendly and protective (playing and looking
     after him)   2   NA
     Not unfriendly   3   DK
     Hostile or jealous   4

124. Does mother think she neglects siblings for him?

> Not at all   0
> In some ways   1
> A great deal   2

125. Does mother think she neglects him for siblings?

> Not at all   0
> In some ways   1
> A great deal   2

126. Would parents place him away from home if there were a vacancy?
State type preferred (e.g., Residential PH School)   NA   0
   DK   1

127. Is he on a waiting list?   NA   0
   DK   1

128. Do parents agree with each other about placement?   NA   0
   DK   1

Attitude to Services

129. How old was the child when the parents first suspected
he was (a) handicapped   years
        (b) backward   ,,   NA

130. To whom did parents go for advice?   GP   1
                                       Hospital   2
                                       M & CW Clinic   3
                                       Faith healers   4
                                       Others   5

Give these in the order in which parents went, how they came to
go to them and advice received.

131. How old was the child when the parents were first told that
he was (a) handicapped   years
        (b) backward   ,,   NA

132. Do the parents think that the doctor should tell the mother
     as soon as he suspects physical or mental defects   1
     as soon as he is sure that the child is handicapped   2
     leave it to her to find out for herself   3
     other   4

133. What happened in this case?

134. When the parents were first told were they able to discuss with
     the doctor what exactly the diagnosis meant and what the child
     would be like and where they could go for advice?   NA   0
                                                                 DK   1

135. When the parents were first told that the child was handicapped
     or backward were they able to discuss with the doctor or social
     worker the pros and cons of school placement and have some
     time for consideration before deciding?   NA   0
                                                        DK   1
                           Had no wish to do so   2

136. Have the parents ever wanted more specialist advice than has been
     given   (a) before ascertainment?   NA   0
                                                 DK   1
                 (b) since ascertainment   NA   0
                                                 DK   1
     If yes, what did they do about it?

137. Do the parents have any worries or fears about what may have been
     the cause of the defect?   NA   0
                                        DK   1
     Describe—

138. Have they discussed this with a doctor at any time?   NA   0
                                                        DK   1
     If so, was this because
                 There was no opportunity to do so   3
                 They did not wish to do so   4

139. Are the parents satisfied that considering his defect the child was reasonably excluded from ordinary school?   NA   o
                                                          DK   1

140. Did they appeal against the exclusion?   NA   o
                                            DK   1

141. Is there any way in which the authorities could make things easier for the parents of handicapped children?
(open question)

PH Schools

142. For how many years has he been attending the school?

143. Does he attend regularly?   NA   o
                                    DK   1

144. Are there travelling difficulties?   NA   o
                                          DK   1

145. What are the main advantages of the PH School? (open question)

146. What are the main disadvantages of the PH School? (open question)

147. If he did not attend would parents be obliged to place him in an institution?   NA   o
                                    DK   1

Home Visitors

148. How many times a year do visitors call to see parents?————
(a) From what organisations?
(b) For what purpose?

149. What do parents think about their coming?
Resent it   o   NA
Don't mind   1   DK
Welcome help   2

150. What is discussed when the visitors come?

151. What do parents think is the purpose of the visits?

152. Can parents think of any way in which home visits could be more helpful?

General

153. To whom would the mother turn if she were ill and could not look after the child?

Relations, friends or neighbours	1
School doctor/nurse	2
GP	3
Social workers	4
(specify ....)	
Other	5

154. If the mother had any worries now that were connected with the child (e.g. his effect on parents' health; relationship with siblings; difficult behaviour), with whom would she discuss them?

Relations, friends or neighbours	1
School doctor/nurse	2
GP	3
Social workers	4
(specify ....)	
Other	5

155. If the parents of a child like yours came to you (the parent) for advice on what to do or how to raise the child, what could you tell them from your own experience?

156. If you (the parent) had it all to do over again in bringing him up, what would you do differently?

APPENDIX II

Teachers' Questionnaire for the National Survey of the Health and Development of Children (May 1959)*

Serial No. ....

Name .... Age ....

I. SCHOOL WORK

1. Please give the following details about this child's present class:

   (a) Number of children on the roll .... children
   of the class
   (b) Sex of children in the class—

   Boys only 1
   Girls only 2
   Mixed 3

   (c) What is the average age of the children
   in this class? ....years.........months
   (d) How many children in the class are under
   13 years of age? ....children
   (e) How many children in the class are over
   14 years of age? ....children

2. Are the children in this school streamed for ability within each year?

   Yes 1
   No 0

   IF 'YES'
   How many streams are there? ....
   In which stream is this child? ....
   If in *Special Class* or *Stream* for backward children please give
   details:
   ....
   ....

* This form should be filled in by the teacher that knows this child best.

3. Please give this child's position in his/her class at the time of the last placing. (If the children in this class are not usually placed, please give an estimate.)

> In top quarter 1
> In the middle half 2
> In the bottom quarter 3

4. Is there any general school subject(s) in which this child's performance is OUTSTANDINGLY GOOD?

> Yes 1
> No 0

IF 'YES' In which subject(s) is he/she outstandingly good?

....

....

5. Is there any general school subject(s) in which this child's performance is OUTSTANDINGLY BAD?

> Yes 1
> No 0

IF 'YES' In which subject(s) is he/she outstandingly bad?

....

6. Has this child been punctual in attending school during the last year?

> Never late unless with good reason......................0
> Sometimes late 1
> Persistently late 2

7. Has this child played truant during the last year?

> Yes, frequently 2
> Yes, occasionally 1
> Never 0

8. Do you consider that this child's school work is adversely affected by any physical disability?

>   Yes 1
>   No ....o

IF 'YES', please give details.
....
....
....
....

9. Do you consider that this child's school work is adversely affected by any factors outside the school (e.g., home circumstances, out of school activities, etc.)?

>   Yes 1
>   No ....o

IF 'YES', please give details.
....
....
....
....
....

10. Are there any *out of school* activities in which this pupil shows exceptional ability?

>   Yes 1
>   No ....o

IF 'YES', please give details.
....
....
....
....
....

11. Please assess this child's ability at games in relation to the other children in the class.

Above average	1
Average	2
Below average	3

12. Do you regard this child as:

Extremely energetic, never tired?	1
Normally energetic?	2
Always tired and 'washed out'?	3

13. (a) Have you discussed this child's education with either of his/her parents during the past year?

Yes, both	1
Yes, mother only	2
Yes, father only	3
Neither	0

(b) To what extent do this child's parents show interest in his/her progress at school?

Very interested	1
Average interest	2
Little or no interest	3

II. CHILD'S ATTITUDE TO SCHOOL WORK

14. Which statement in each group *best* describes this child?

(a) A very hard worker	1
Average—works moderately well	2
A poor worker or lazy	3
(b) One with high power of concentration	1
Average—concentrates moderately well	2
Little or no power of sustained concentration	3

    (c) Extremely neat and tidy in
        class work 1
        Average—moderately neat
        and tidy 2
        Very untidy in class work 3
    (d) Seldom or never disobedient 1
        Sometimes disobedient 2
        Frequently disobedient 3
    (e) Seldom or never difficult to
        discipline 1
        Sometimes difficult to
        discipline 2
        Frequently difficult to
        discipline 3
    (f) Seldom or never restless in class 1
        Sometimes restless in class 2
        Frequently restless in class 3
    (g) Seldom or never daydreams
        in class 1
        Sometimes daydreams in class 2
        Frequently daydreams in class 3
    (h) Seldom or never cribs 1
        Sometimes cribs 2
        Frequently cribs 3
    (i) Seldom or never evades the
        truth to keep out of trouble 1
        Sometimes evades the truth to
        keep out of trouble 2
        Frequently evades the truth to
        keep out of trouble 3

III. BEHAVIOUR

15. Which statement in each group *best* describes this child?
    (a) Very popular with other children 1
        Of average popularity 2
        Tends to be ignored by other
        children 3

(b) Liable to get unduly rough during
playtime 1
Takes a normal part in rough
games 2
Rather frightened of rough games 3

(c) Avoids attention, hates being in
the limelight 1
Does not unduly avoid or seek
attention 2
Shows off; seeks attention 3

(d) A dare-devil 1
As cautious as the average child 2
Extremely fearful 3

(e) Over-competitive with other
children 1
Normally competitive 2
Diffident about competing with
other children 3

(f) Unusually happy and contented
child 1
Generally cheerful and in good
humour 2
Usually gloomy and sad 3

(g) A quarrelsome and aggressive child 1
Average—not particularly
quarrelsome 2
A timid child 3

(h) Makes friends extremely easily 1
Takes usual amount of time to
make friends 2
Does not seem able to make friends 3

IV. HABITS

16. Has this child frequently shown any of the following habits or
mannerisms?

(a) Nail biting	Yes	....	1
	No	....	0
(b) Nose picking	Yes	....	1
	No	....	0
(c) Thumb or finger sucking	Yes	....	1
	No	....	0
(d) Picking Sores	Yes	....	1
	No	....	0
(e) Stammering	Yes	....	1
	No	....	0
(f) Nervous twitches or grimaces	Yes	....	1
	No	....	0

Please comment if any of these habits are shown to an extreme degree.

....

17. Has this child, to your knowledge, any puzzling or inexplicable habits; or are there ritualistic acts which he finds it essential to perform without knowing why, such as touching every desk or person passed, or smelling every object come across?

> Yes 1
> No 0

IF 'YES', what are these habits?

....
....
....
....
....

18. Has this child, to your knowledge, an obsession about cleanliness or a morbid pre-occupation with any other idea or condition?

> Yes 1
> No 0

IF 'YES', please specify.

....
....

19. Has this child, to your knowledge, any phobias—i.e. is there any object, person or situation of which he is unreasonably afraid?

Yes 1
No 0

IF 'YES', please specify.

....
....
....
....

20. Would you describe this child as an anxious child—i.e. apprehensive, worrying and fearful?

Not at all anxious 0
Somewhat anxious................. 1
Very anxious 2

21. Does this child show extreme changes of mood, swinging between periods of elation and great activity and periods of gloominess and lethargy?

Yes 1
No 0

22. How does this child react to criticism or punishment?

Tends to become unduly resentful 1
Tends to become unduly miserable or worried 2
Normal attitude to criticism and punishment 0

23. Taking this child's behaviour and relationships with other children as a whole, would you say he/she is—

	Not at all	Somewhat	Very
Sensitive or highly strung	0	1	2
Shy or withdrawn	0	1	2
Aggressive	0	1	2
Other, namely	–	1	2

....
....

24. Please comment on any problems of adjustment or conduct which are or might be a cause of concern.

....
....
....
....
....

V. SCHOOL ATTENDANCE

25. Please give the following details of this child's school attendance during the past year.

	Attendancies made by this child ($\frac{1}{2}$ days)	Attendancies that could have been made ($\frac{1}{2}$ days)
Winter term		
Spring term		
Summer term		

Teacher's Name ....
(Mr, Mrs, Miss)

How well do you know this child?

Very well	1
Moderately well	2
Not very well	3

Date ....

APPENDIX III A

Emotional Difficulties in the Children:
Method of Scoring from the Survey Questionnaire

Questions	Scored responses	Points
NERVOUS DISORDERS		
88. Fears	2 extremely fearful or timid 3 rather fearful or timid	1
89. Withdrawal	2 (solitary)	1
86. Apathy	2 or 3 (apathetic or underactive)	1
85. Temperament and conduct	3 or 6 (very sensitive or very shy)	1
84. Attitude to disability	1 or 2 (having considerable difficulties or unable to cope unaided)	1
Total points		5
HABIT DISORDERS		
9. Speech defects	3 (stammering)	1
98. Disturbed sleep	1	1
97. Bad Habits		7
(a) Comfort habits	0, 1, 3 (sucking, rocking, other. Specify)	
(b) Tension habits	4, 5, 6, 7 (picking, biting, tics head-banging)	
36. Incontinence	1	1
Total points		10

BEHAVIOUR DISORDERS

90. Defiance	4 or 5 (fairly often or almost always)	1
91. Tantrums	4 or 5 (daily or constantly)	1
92. Bullying	4 (fairly often)	1
93. Aggressiveness (physical)	4 (fairly often)	1
94. Destructiveness	4 (fairly often)	1
121. Jealousy	1	1
100. Attention-seeking	0 (constantly demands attention)	1
50. Serious trouble	1	1
85. Aggressiveness (temperament)	8 or 9 (somewhat or very aggressive)	1
Total points		9
Grand total: signs of failure to adjust		24

APPENDIX III B

Emotional Difficulties in the Children:
Method of scoring from the teachers' questionnaire

Questions	Scored responses	Points

NERVOUS DISORDERS

14. Attitude to school work
    (g) Daydreaming — 3 (frequently daydreams) — 1

15. Behaviour
    (c) Attention — 1 (avoids attention, hates being in limelight) — 1
    (d) Fear — 3 (extremely fearful) — 1
    (f) Humour — 3 (usually gloomy and sad) — 1
    (h) Friendships — 3 (does not seem able to make friends) — 1

20. Anxiety — 1 or 2 (somewhat anxious or very anxious) — 1

22. Reaction to criticism or punishment — 2 (unduly miserable or worried) — 1

    Total points — 7

HABIT DISORDERS

16. Habits — Nail-biting, nose-picking, thumb- or finger-sucking, picking sores, stammering, nervous twitches or grimaces — 6

    Total points — 6

BEHAVIOUR DISORDERS

14. Attitude to school work
    (d) Obedience   3 (frequently disobedient)   1
    (e) Discipline   3 (frequently difficult to discipline)   1
    (f) Restlessness   3 (frequently restless in class)   1
    (h) Cribbing   3 (frequently cribs)   1
    (i) Truthfulness   3 (frequently evades the truth to keep out of trouble)   1

15. Behaviour
    (b) Rough games   1 (liable to get unduly rough during playtime)   1
    (c) Attention-seeking   3 (shows off; seeks attention)   1
    (d) Fear   1 (a dare-devil)   1
    (e) Competitiveness   1 (over-competitive with other children)   1
    (g) Aggressiveness   1 (a quarrelsome and aggressive child)   1

22. Reaction to criticism or punishment   1 (tends to become unduly resentful)   1

Total points   11

Grand total: signs of failure to adjust   24

APPENDIX III C

INTERPRETATION OF SCORING

It will be seen that the responses are not weighted. Thus, to Question 88 in the survey questionnaire, for example, 'Is he nervous or timid (afraid of noises, of the dark, shy of strangers, afraid to venture out of the house alone)?', responses 2 ('extremely nervous even in a familiar environment') and 3 ('rather nervous or timid') both score one point. Similarly, to item 20 in the teachers' questionnaire, 'Would you describe this child as an anxious child?', both 'somewhat anxious' and 'very anxious' score one point.

Scores from the two questionnaires on the children's adjustment to their handicaps were interpreted as shown below.

Emotional difficulties	Score out of 24	Interpretation
Normal	0–1	Normal reactions
Slight	2–3	Slight emotional difficulties relative to handicap
Moderate	4–5	Moderately severe emotional difficulties and failure to adjust
Severe	6 or over	Severe emotional difficulties and failure to adjust

APPENDIX IV

Assessment of parents' emotional difficulties

The adjustment of the parents to the handicap was evaluated in terms of:

(i) *over-anxiety*, over-protection, depression
(ii) *rejection*, friction, aggression
(iii) *normal reaction*, acceptance of handicap, adjustment

The method of scoring *over-anxiety* is shown below.

Questions	Scored responses	Points
Survey questionnaire		
73. Depression (mother)	2 or 3 (frequently or always)	1
71. Anxiety (father)	1 or 2	1
74. Anxiety (mother)	1	1
75. Insomnia (mother)	1	1
76. Tension (mother)	1	1
78. Fatigue (mother)	1	1
117. Attitude to disability (mother)	1 or 2 (having difficulty in coping with the handicap or unable to cope unaided)	1
118. Attitude to disability (father)	1 or 2	1
Total points		8

The method of scoring *rejection* is shown below.

Questions	Scored responses	Points
Survey questionnaire		
101. Separation or divorce	(1)	1
102. Quarrels about child	(1a)	1
107. Mother ashamed and embarrassed, i.e. avoids people or rarely takes him out	(2 or 3)	1
108. Father ashamed and embarrassed, i.e. avoids people or rarely takes him out.	(2 or 3)	1
Total points		4

Questions	Scored responses	Points
Teachers' questionnaire		
13a. Discussion with parents	(0 none)	1
13b. Interest in progress	(3, little or none)	1
9. Adverse home circs.	(1)	1
24. Adverse comments adjustment	(open question)	1
Total points		4

APPENDIX V

Emotional Adjustment of Siblings

Questions	Scored responses	Families affected
119. Does the child's presence impede their work or play?	1 (yes)	6
120. Does his presence interfere with their social relationships (e.g. neighbours won't play with them, unable to bring friends home)?	1 (yes)	6
121. Does the child ill-treat siblings (e.g. baby)?	1 (yes)	6
122. Do they show marked jealousy or neurotic symptoms which can be related to him?	1 (yes)	13
124. Does mother think she neglects siblings for him?	1 (in some ways)	5
125. Does mother think she neglects him for siblings?	1 (in some ways)	1
123. What is their attitude to him	2 (friendly and protective, playing with and looking after him) 3 (not unfriendly) 4 (hostile or jealous)	26 ⎫ 5 ⎬ 37 6 ⎭

APPENDIX VI

Differences Between Parents' and Teachers' Assessments of the Children's Emotional Difficulties

Sixteen Cases in which the Teachers' Estimates were Lower

In six instances the difference between the assessment of the parent and the assessment of the teacher was one point only, presumably accounted for by the different conditions at home and at school.

In four other cases, where the differences amounted to nine, six, six and five points respectively, the mothers were known to be acutely anxious (three were attending a child guidance clinic, and one a psychiatrist).

In three instances where the teacher's estimate was lower by four points, the mothers had considerable difficulties with the children at home: two were cerebral palsy cases, one an intelligent and frustrated child, the other adversely affected by marked friction between the parents; the third child was the haemangioma who was out of control at home. These children were now behaving quite well at school.

In three cases, where the differences were three, three and two, the difficulties were similar but less marked.

Twenty-seven Cases in which the Teachers' Estimates were Higher

In seven cases the teacher's assessment was considerably higher than the mother's (four points or more). In six of these, where the discrepancies between the scores were eleven, ten, six, five and four points respectively, there were a variety of reasons why the mothers appeared to underestimate their children's difficulties.

For example, the teacher's estimate was eleven points higher in the case of a child with severe haemophilia; the child should have been attending a child guidance clinic, with a 'chronic anxiety state of a fairly severe degree', but the mother was unable to accept the treatment. There were ten points between the assessments in respect of a child with severe cerebral palsy with epilepsy and mental retardation; the mother was so delighted with the child's progress (she had been told that he would be blind and deaf, and never off his back) that she quite obviously under-estimated his difficulties. In a third case, where the difference was five points, the mother appeared to be of rather low intelligence; she was so little concerned over the child's handicap that she was constantly missing his hospital appointments. The four other cases in this group could be explained in somewhat similar ways.

Among the remaining twenty cases, where the disparity between the scores was less marked, two mothers appeared to underestimate their children's difficulties because they wanted them to return to normal schools.

Since the teachers' assessments were considered to be more objective and reliable than the mothers', they were used as the measure of the children's failure to adjust in all cases in which differences occurred, except for the two instances described below.

In Case 35, the mother's assessment was six and the teacher's two. This was the child with severe athetoid spastic paraplegia, with dysarthria, who was referred to a child guidance clinic for advice about residential placement. She was an intelligent and frustrated child, but fully occupied and happy in school. At home, however, there were a number of emotion-ally disturbing factors: friction between the maternal grandmother, who shared the flat, and the father; some lack of marital harmony; a mother who remarked 'I would have liked a large family, and envy other people's families'.

In the second case (49), one of the children with haemophilia, the mother assessed the symptoms of maladjustment at nine points and the teacher at three. The child appeared reasonably happy and well adjusted at school, although the teacher considered him 'somewhat sensitive and highly strung'. His mother stated that at home, 'he withdraws and retreats to bed'. This child wrapped himself up in his baby shawl each night to go to sleep. There were considerable marital difficulties. The mother said that she would 'break the marrriage' if she did not feel that a broken home would be bad for him.

APPENDIX VII

Differences Between Assessments of Parental Rejection from the Survey and the Teachers' Questionnaire

As was noted in Chapter 7, in thirty-nine cases the scores from the two questionnaires were either the same or differed by only one point.

In five of the remaining nine cases, the difference between the estimates was two points. (In four of these the score from the teachers' questionnaire was higher; in one instance the score from the survey questionnaire was higher.)

In the remaining four cases, the difference between the estimates was three points (higher from the teachers' questionnaire in three cases and from the survey questionnaire in one case). These four cases are described briefly below.

One (Case 7) has already been noted: the child was illegitimate and was brought up by the grandparents. In a second instance (Case 15), the teacher observed indications of rejection which were not acknowledged by the parents, who were struggling not very successfully, to manage a large family. The third case (Case 14) was the only one in which the child was considered by the teacher to be grossly over-protected; the prognosis was fatal and the mother was unable to adjust to the situation. In the fourth instance (Case 19), where the score from the survey questionnaire was three points higher, the mother freely admitted her own and her husband's partial rejection, friction, and temporary separation.

APPENDIX VIII. Adjustment tables

TABLE A. 12 cases of normal or slight emotional difficulties in both the child and the parents.

Case no.	Handicap	Severity	Prognosis*	Rejection scores	Parental Reactions Masked or open	Marital relations†	Hosp. no.	Admis. duration (wks)
4	Poliomyelitis (Shoulder)	Moderate	Fair	—	Masked	Second Marriage (Not known)	2	66
7	Spastic Hemiplegia	Moderate	Fair	Severe (Mother)	Open (Mother)	Not known	2	3
8	TB spine (healed)	Slight	Good	Moderate	Open	Poor	1	200
20	Chronic osteomyelitis	Slight	Good	—	—	—	26	98
23	Achondro-plasia	Slight	Fair	Slight	Masked	Good	—	—
26	Athetoid paraplegia	Severe	Fair	—	—	Good	1	½
28	Spastic paraplegia	Moderate	Fair	—	—	Good	5	24
29	Poliomyelitis (R. leg)	Slight	Fair	Severe (Mother)	Open (Mother)	Broken	3	32
34	Spastic monoplegia	Slight	Fair	—	—	Good	2	3½
40	Poliomyelitis (R. leg)	Slight	Fair	Slight	Open	—	2	107
43	Poliomyelitis (R. leg)	Slight	Fair	Slight	Open	—	2	107
46	Haemophilia	Severe	Poor	—	Open (Adoption)	—	6	3

* *Prognosis:* 'good' in relation to life and normal achievement; 'fair' in relation to normal achievement; 'poor' in relation to life (longevity) only.
† *Marital Relations:* no comment made unless the home circumstances were well known and significant for the child.

196

Appendix VIII

Comments

Mother: assessed as masked rejection; indications of over-anxiety, ? guilt. Marital friction.
Child: 'Too quiet' (Mother)
    'Shy or withdrawn' (Teacher)

Mother: open rejection; child brought up by grandparents; affectionate relations.
Child: 'Timid but improving' (Teacher).

Mother: open rejection; child 4 years in hospital until better living accommodation.
Child: 'Doesn't show affection' (Mother).

Mother: no apparent rejection; apparently well adjusted. Father had severe depression.
Child: attending child guidance for enuresis (with brother), but psychiatrist considers child reasonably well adjusted.

Mother: partially masked rejection. Initial open rejection and continuing feelings of shame and guilt.
Child: 'Occasional tantrums' (Mother); feeding difficulties in school (Teacher).

Mother: no apparent rejection. Appeared well adjusted; father had severe depression; sibling emotional problems.
Child: apparently well adjusted.

Mother: no apparent rejection; apparently well adjusted.
Child: apparently well adjusted.

Mother: open rejection (deserted); father apparently well adjusted, affectionate and protective.
Child: initial emotional problems, pilfering in school, nocturnal enuresis; subsequently improving.

Mother: no apparent rejection; apparently well adjusted.
Child: ditto.

Mother: open rejection (slight and admitted).
Child shows some anxiety and frustration; ? withdrawn.

Mother: open rejection (failure to visit in hospital); father suffered anxiety symptoms.
Child: 'Temperamental and difficult'; resents crutches. 'Very nervous when put out of hospital' (Mother); now improving.

Mother: open initial rejection (adopted). No apparent rejection by adoptive mother; apparently well adjusted.
Child: apparently well adjusted.

(a) Severity	(b) Prognosis	(c) Parental reaction	(d) Marital relations	(e) Hospital admissions
severe 2	poor 1	no rejection 4	broken 1	none—26 times
moderate 3	fair 9	open rejection 6 (1 inclg. adoption)	poor 1	Duration
slight 7	good 2	Masked rejection 2	good 4	0–200 weeks
			not known 6	

197

TABLE B. 10 cases. Normal or slight emotional difficulties in the child, moderately severe, or severe in the parents

Case no.	Handicap	Severity	Prognosis	Rejection scores	Parental Reactions Masked or open	Marital relations	Hosp. no.	Admis. duration (wks.)
1	Urethral stricture	Severe	Poor	—	—	—	8	61
5	Spastic paraplegia	Severe	Fair	Moderate	Open	Poor	7	28
10	Ataxic paraplegia	Moderate	Good	Slight	Open (Father)	Broken	1	2
11	Haemophilia	Severe	Poor	—	—	Poor	15	59
15	Poliomyelitis	Moderate	Fair	Severe	Open	Poor	2	56
19	Multiple congenital defects	Severe	Poor	Severe (Father)	Open (Father)	Poor	4	26
36	Poliomyelitis	Severe	Fair	—	—	—	2	52
37	Bilateral talipes	Slight	Good	Slight	Open (Father)	Poor	5	17
39	Poliomyelitis (L. leg)	Slight	Good	Slight	Open (Father)	Poor	2	100
48	Epispadias	Severe	Poor	Slight	Open	—	6	26

Comments

Mother anxious and depressed, some guilt feelings, only partially accepted poor prognosis; child had recurrent hospitalization.

Mother anxious, some rejection and shame; raised question of residential school; marked marital friction; child had severe speech defect; child guidance considered.

Parents divorced (father deserted); mother severely anxious; domestic and housing difficulties.

Family had three haemophilic boys; marital relationship deteriorated. Some guilt feelings. Child developing emotional problems following family's move to country area.

Large family; financial difficulties.

Child retarded; marital disharmony; father deserted temporarily; sibling jealousy.

Mother agoraphobia, over-protective, guilt feelings.

Father previously suffered from shell shock, frequently unemployed, rejection ('takes no part in caring for child'); child retarded.

Parents temporarily separated; large family; child slightly aggressive.

Mother in poor health; admitted some shame and embarrassment; underestimated child's anxiety. Child has learning difficulties; some deep anxieties.

SUMMARY:

(a) *Severity*	(b) *Prognosis*	(c) *Parental reactions*	(d) *Marital relations*	(e) *Hospital admissions*
severe 6	poor 4	no rejection 3	broken 1	1–15 times
moderate 2	fair 3	open rejection 7	poor 6	*Duration*
slight 2	good 3	masked rejection –	not known 3	2–100 weeks

TABLE C. 10 cases. Moderately severe or severe emotional difficulties in the child, normal or slight in the parents.

Case no.	Handicap	Severity	Prognosis	Rejection scores	Parental Reactions Masked or open	Marital relations	Hosp. no.	Admis. duration (wks)
2	Spastic hemiplegia	Severe	Fair	Moderate	Open	Poor	2	23
3	Bilateral talipes	Slight	Good	Moderate	Open	Poor	4	22
17	Cerebral ataxia	Slight	Fair	—	Masked	—	5	23
18	Spastic hemiplegia	Slight	Fair	—	Masked	—	5	14½
21	Spastic paraplegia	Moderate	Fair	Slight	Open	—	22	45
25	Epilepsy	Slight	Good	—	Masked	—	6	13
27	Spastic hemiplegia	Slight	Fair	Slight	Open	Broken	—	—
30	Muscular dystrophy	Severe	Poor	—	Death	—	3	2
33	Cerebral ataxia	Severe	Poor	Slight	Open	—	4	31
44	Spastic paraplegia	Slight	Fair	—	Masked	—	1	5

Comments

Child severely anxious (child guidance at mother's request); rejected by family, including grandparents (emigration refused on account of handicap); maternal anxiety masked at interview; mother in ill health; sibling anxiety.

Both parents deserted; child brought up by grandparents; friction between mother and grandparents.

Mother depressed, some apparent anxiety because of handicap and delay in diagnosis; assessed as some rejection; sibling jealousy.

Mother afraid of another pregnancy. Anxiety and rejection masked. Child timid and anxious.

Parents unable to accept child's mental retardation at first; attitude improved with casework; child referred for psychiatric help.

Mother's severe anxiety masked; she had had breakdown and worried excessively over child's food; unable to accept child's mental retardation. Teacher describes him as very anxious.

Mother fairly well adjusted; father deserted; child severely anxious (loss of father).

Maternal 'rejection' through death; aunt (and father) well adjusted.

Mother depressed; guilt feelings, anxiety and rejection masked; sibling jealousy.

Mother ignores handicap and child; leaves him to care of grandmother; fails to keep treatment appointments.

SUMMARY:

(a) *Severity*	(b) *Prognosis*	(c) *Parental reactions*	(d) *Marital relations*	(e) *Hospital admissions*
severe 3	poor 2	rejection open 5 (+1 death)	broken 1	none—22 times
moderate 1	fair 6	rejection masked 4	poor 2	*Duration*
slight 6	good 2		not known 7	0–45 weeks

TABLE D. 12 cases. Moderately severe or severe emotional difficulties in both the child and the parents

Case no.	Handicap	Severity	Prognosis	Rejection scores	Parental Reactions Masked or open	Marital relations	Hosp. no.	Admis. duration (wks.)
9	Multiple Congenital defects	Severe	Poor	Slight	Open	Widow (broken)	16	45½
12	Fallot's tetralogy	Severe	Poor	Slight	Masked	Poor	6	14
13	Spinal tumour	Severe	Poor	Severe (Father)	Open (Father)	Poor	2	15
16	Spastic hemiplegia	Slight	Fair	—	—	Poor	4	10
22	Spastic paraplegia	Moderate	Fair	—	—	Poor	1	1
31	Atrial septal defect	Severe	Fair	Moderate	Open	—	—	—
35	Spastic paraplegia	Severe	Fair	Slight	Masked	Poor	1	5
38	Spastic hemiplegia	Severe	Fair	Slight	Masked	—	7	13
42	Haemophilia	Severe	Poor	Moderate	Open	Poor	30	58
45	Suspected ventricular septal defect	Slight	Good	—	—	—	2	17
49	Haemophilia	Severe	Poor	Slight	Open	Poor	15	22
50	Poliomyelitis	Moderate	Fair	Moderate	Open	—	1	54

Comments

Mother under psychiatrist; previous marital friction (severe); father died when child aged 4. Child retarded.

Parents severely anxious; partially masked rejection (prognosis fatal), unable to accept handicap. Child feels unaccepted.

Marital disharmony; father chronic alcoholic (rejection); mother under hospital (neurosis). Child timid and withdrawn; regular casework.

Child affected by marked marital friction; anxious and timid mother afraid of future pregnancy (previous illegitimate child); guilt and over-protection.

Mother had had two thyroid operations; over-protective; child timid and solitary.

Both parents rejecting; mother tense, unable to accept regular child guidance; child depressed; sibling jealousy.

Some partially masked rejection; fear of future pregnancy; child intelligent and frustrated. Regular casework (child guidance considered).

Mother unable to accept mental retardation; father an invalid; child timid and anxious.

Marital friction; mother depressed, guilt feelings. Child aggressive, referred for child guidance.

Mother agoraphobia; under psychiatric treatment. Child afraid of dark; aggressive temper tantrums, etc. Sibling jealousy.

Marital disharmony; mother anxious and aggressive; father rejecting; child severely anxious, remedial teaching at child guidance clinic.

Mother unable to cope; sibling jealousy.

SUMMARY:

(a) *Severity*	(b) *Prognosis*	(c) *Parental reactions*	(d) *Marital relations*	(e) *Hospital admissions*
severe 8	poor 5	no rejection 3	broken 1 (widow)	none—30 times
moderate 2	fair 6	rejection open 6	poor 7	*Duration*
slight 2	good 1	rejection masked 3	not known 4	0–58 weeks

TABLE E. 6 cases. Moderately severe or severe emotional difficulties in the whole family (parents, handicapped child, and siblings)

Case no.	Handicap	Severity	Prognosis	Rejection scores	Parental Reactions Masked or open	Marital relations	Hosp. no.	Admis. duration (wks.)
6	Spastic diplegia	Moderate	Fair	Severe	Open	Broken	1	1
14	Brain tumour	Severe	Poor	Severe	Open	—	1	3
24	Haemangioma, R. hemiplegia	Severe	Poor	Severe	Open	Poor	10	18½
32	Spastic Hemiplegia	Moderate	Fair	Slight	Open	—	5	3
41	Fallot's tetralogy	Severe	Poor	—	Masked	—	4	18
47	Muscular dystrophy	Severe	Poor	Slight	Open (Father)	Poor	1	3

Appendix VIII

Comments

Father deserted; mother opposed to child guidance; sibling jealousy.

Mother depressed, over-protective (prognosis fatal). Sibling maladjustment.

Maternal rejection; child retarded, under hospital psychiatric dept. Poor home conditions. Severe sibling anxiety.

Mother frequent asthmatic attacks; child affected by mother's anxiety. Sibling jealousy.

Mother chronic anxiety, over-protective, some masked rejection; child under hospital psychiatric dept. Severe sibling disturbance.

Father unable to accept child's handicap (rejection). Child severely anxious, child guidance; sibling difficulties (2 children with muscular dystrophy).

SUMMARY:

(a) *Severity*	(b) *Prognosis*	(c) *Parental reactions*	(d) *Marital relations*	(e) *Hospital admissions*
severe 4	poor 4	rejection open 5	broken 1	1–10 times
moderate 2	fair 2	rejection masked 1	poor 2	*Duration*
			not known 3	1–18½ weeks

INDEX